ALSO BY TONY JUDT

Ill Fares the Land

Reappraisals: Reflections on the
Forgotten Twentieth Century

Postwar: A History of
Europe Since 1945

The Politics of Retribution in Europe
(with Jan Gross and István Deák)

The Burden of Responsibility:
Blum, Camus, Aron, and the
French Twentieth Century

Language, Nation and State:
Identity Politics in a Multilingual Age
(edited with Denis Lacorne)

A Grand Illusion?:
An Essay on Europe

Past Imperfect:
French Intellectuals, 1944–1956

Marxism and the French Left:
Studies on Labour and
Politics in France 1930–1982

Resistance and Revolution

In Mediterranean Europe 1939–1948

Socialism in Provence 1871–1914:
A Study in the Origins of the
Modern French Left

La reconstruction du Parti
Socialiste 1921–1926

The Memory Chalet

Tony Judt

WILLIAM HEINEMANN: LONDON

Published by William Heinemann 2010

2 4 6 8 10 9 7 5 3 1

First published in Great Britain in 2010 by
William Heinemann
Random House, 20 Vauxhall Bridge Road,
London SW1V 2SA

www.rbooks.co.uk

Addresses for companies within The Random House Group Limited can be found at:
www.randomhouse.co.uk/offices.htm

The Random House Group Limited Reg. No. 954009

A CIP catalogue record for this book
is available from the British Library

ISBN 9780434020966

The Random House Group Limited supports The Forest Stewardship
Council (FSC), the leading international forest certification organisation. All our
titles that are printed on Greenpeace approved FSC certified paper carry the FSC logo.
Our paper procurement policy can be found at:
www.rbooks.co.uk/environment

Mixed Sources
Product group from well-managed
forests and other controlled sources
www.fsc.org Cert no. TT-COC-2139
© 1996 Forest Stewardship Council

Designed by Claire Naylon Vaccaro

Printed and bound in Great Britain by
Clays Ltd, St Ives Plc

For Jennifer, Daniel and Nicholas

Contents

Part Three

Envoi

Preface

The essays in this little book were never intended for publication. I started writing them for my own satisfaction—and at the encouragement of Timothy Garton Ash, who urged me to turn to advantage the increasingly internal reference of my own thoughts. I do not think that I had any idea what it was I was embarking upon, and I am grateful to Tim for his confident support of the initial scribblings that resulted.

About halfway through the writing of these *feuilletons* I showed one or two of them to my agents at the Wylie Agency, as well as to Robert Silvers at the *New York Review of Books* and was heartened at their enthusiasm. However, this raised an ethical question for me. Because I did not write them with the view to immediate publication, these short pieces never benefitted from an internal editor—or, more precisely, a private censor. Where they spoke of my parents or my childhood, of ex-wives and present colleagues, I let them speak. This has the merit of directness; I hope it will not cause offense.

I have not altered or rephrased any of the original texts, which were written with the help and collaboration of my long-time colleague Eugene Rusyn. Reading them over, I see that I have been quite open and occasionally even critical of those I love, whereas I was judiciously silent for the most part regarding people of whom I have retained a less-than-affectionate regard. Doubtless this is how it should be. I do hope that my parents, my wife and above all my children will read in these exercises in fond recall further evidence of my abiding love for them all.

I

The Memory Chalet

For me the word "chalet" conjures up a very distinctive image. It brings to mind a small *pensione*, a family hotel in the unfashionable village of Chesières, at the foot of the well-heeled Villars ski region in French-speaking Switzerland. We must have spent a winter holiday there in 1957 or '58. The skiing—or in my case, sledding—cannot have been very memorable: I recall only that my parents and uncle used to trudge over the icy foot bridge and on up to the ski lifts, spending the day there but abjuring the fleshpots of the *après-ski* in favor of a quiet evening in the chalet.

For me this was always the best part of a winter holiday: the repetitive snow-bound entertainment abandoned by early afternoon for heavy armchairs, warm wine, solid country food, and long evenings in the open lounge decompressing among strangers. But what strangers! The curiosity of the little *pensione* in Chesières lay in its apparent attraction to down-at-heel British actors vacationing in the distant, indifferent shadow of their more successful fellows farther up the mountain.

The second evening we were there, the dining room was graced with a volley of sexual epithets that brought my mother to her feet. No stranger to bad language—she was raised within earshot of the old West India Docks—she had been apprenticed out of her class into the polite limbo of ladies hairdressing and had no intention of exposing her family to such filth.

Mrs. Judt duly marched across to the offending table and asked that they desist: there were children present. Since my sister was not yet eighteen months, and I was the only other child in the hotel, this request was presumably advanced for my benefit. The young—and, as I later surmised, unemployed—actors who were responsible for the outburst immediately apologized and invited us to join them for dessert.

They were a marvelous crew, not least to the all-seeing (and all-hearing) ten-year-old now placed in their midst. All were unknown at this point, though some would go on to an illustrious future: Alan Badel, not yet a prominent Shakespearean actor with a respectable filmography to his credit (*Day of the Jackal*); but above all the irrepressible Rachel Roberts, soon to become the iconic disillusioned working-class wife of the greatest British postwar movies (*Saturday*

Night and Sunday Morning, This Sporting Life, O Lucky Man!).
It was Roberts who took me under her wing, muttering un-
repeatable imprecations in a whisky-fueled baritone that left
me with few illusions as to her future, though a certain confusion regarding my own. Over the course of that vacation
she taught me poker, assorted card tricks, and more bad language than I have had time to forget.

Perhaps for this reason, the little Swiss hotel on Chesières's high street has a fonder as well as a deeper place in
my memory than other doubtless identical wooden construc-
tions where I have slept over the years. We only stayed there
for ten days or so, and I have returned on just one brief
occasion. But I can describe even today the intimate style of
the place.

There were few excrescences of indulgence: you entered on a mezzanine level separating a small basement area
from the business rooms of the main floor—the point of this
mezzanine being to segregate the dripping paraphernalia of
outdoor sport (skis, boots, sticks, jackets, sleds, etc.) from the
cozy, dry ambiance of the public rooms. The latter, set to
both sides of the reception desk, had large, attractive windows giving on to the main road of the village and the steep
gorges surrounding it. Behind them in turn were the kitchens
and other service spaces, obscured by a broad and unusually
steep staircase leading to the bedroom floor.

The latter divided neatly and perhaps intentionally into
the better-furnished sleeping accommodation to the left and

the smaller, single, waterless rooms farther along, leading in their turn to a narrow set of steps culminating in an attic floor preserved for employees (except at the height of the season). I have not checked, but I doubt whether there were more than twelve rooms for rent, in addition to the three public areas and the common spaces surrounding them. This was a small hotel for small families of modest means, set in an unpretentious village with no ambitions above its geographical station in life. There must be ten thousand such hostelries in Switzerland: I just happen to have a near-perfect visual recollection of one of them.

Except as a pleasant reminder of contented memories, I doubt whether I gave the Chesières chalet a second thought for much of the ensuing fifty years. And yet when I was diagnosed with amyotrophic lateral sclerosis (ALS) in 2008 and quickly came to understand that I would most likely not travel again—indeed, would be very fortunate if I were even in a position to write about my travels—it was the Chesières hotel that came insistently to mind. Why?

The salient quality of this particular neurodegenerative disorder is that it leaves your mind clear to reflect upon past, present, and future, but steadily deprives you of any means of converting those reflections into words. First you can no longer write independently, requiring either an assistant or a machine in order to record your thoughts. Then your legs fail and you cannot take in new experiences, except at the cost of such logistical complexity that the mere fact of mobility becomes the object of attention rather than the benefits that mobility itself can confer.

Next you begin to lose your voice: not just in the metaphorical sense of having to speak through assorted mechanical or human intermediaries, but quite literally in that the diaphragm muscles can no longer pump sufficient air across your vocal cords to furnish them with the variety of pressure required to express meaningful sound. By this point you are almost certainly quadriplegic and condemned to long hours of silent immobility, whether or not in the presence of others.

For someone wishing to remain a communicator of words and concepts, this poses an unusual challenge. Gone is the yellow pad, with its now useless pencil. Gone the refreshing walk in the park or workout in the gym, where ideas and sequences fall into place as if by natural selection. Gone too are productive exchanges with close friends—even at the midpoint of decline from ALS, the victim is usually thinking far faster than he can form words, so that conversation itself becomes partial, frustrating, and ultimately self-defeating.

I think I came across the answer to this dilemma quite by chance. I realized, some months into the disease, that I was writing whole stories in my head in the course of the night. Doubtless I was seeking oblivion, replacing galumphing sheep with narrative complexity to comparable effect. But in the course of these little exercises, I realized that I was reconstructing—LEGO-like—interwoven segments of my own past which I had never previously thought of as related. This in itself was no great achievement: the streams of consciousness that would carry me from a steam engine to my German language class, from the carefully constructed route lines of London's country buses to the history of interwar town planning—were easy enough to furrow and thence follow in all manner of interesting directions. But how should I recapture those half-buried tracks the following day?

It was here that nostalgic recollections of happier days spent in cozy central European villages began to play a more practical role. I had long been fascinated by the mnemonic devices employed by early-modern thinkers and travelers to store and recall detail and description: these are beautifully depicted in the Renaissance essays of Frances Yates—and more recently in Jonathan Spence's account of an Italian traveler to medieval China, *The Memory Palace of Matteo Ricci*.

Such would-be memorizers did not build mere hostelries or residences in which to house their knowledge: they built *palaces*. However, I had no desire to construct palaces in my head. The real thing had always struck me as somehow indulgent: from Wolsey's Hampton Court to Louis XIV's Versailles, such extravagances were always intended to impress rather than to serve. I could no more have imagined in my still and silent nights such a memory palace than I could have sewn myself a star-spangled suit of pantaloon and vest. But if not a memory palace, why not a memory chalet?

The advantage of a chalet lay not only in the fact that I

could envisage it in very considerable and realistic detail—
from the snow rail by the doorstep to the inner window keeping the Valaison winds at bay—but that it was a place I would
want to visit again and again. In order for a memory palace to
work as a storehouse of infinitely reorganized and regrouped
recollections, it needs to be a building of extraordinary appeal,
if only for one person. Each night, for days, weeks, months,
and now well over a year, I have returned to that chalet. I
have passed through its familiar short corridors with their
worn stone steps and settled into one of two or perhaps three
armchairs—conveniently unoccupied by others. And thence,
the wish fathering the thought with reasonably unerring reli-
ability, I have conjured up, sorted out, and ordered a story or
an argument or an example that I plan to use in something I
shall write the following day.

What then? Here is where the chalet transforms itself
from a mnemonic trigger to a storage device. Once I know
roughly what I want to say and a sequence in which it is best
said, I leave the armchair and go back to the door of the chalet itself. From here I retrace my steps, usually from the first
storage closet—for skis, let's say—toward ever more substantial spaces: the bar, the dining room, the lounge, the
old-fashioned wooden key rack pinned under the cuckoo
clock, the rather random collection of books straggling up
the back staircase, and thence to one of any number of bedrooms. To each of these locations has been assigned a staging
point in a narrative, say, or perhaps an illustrative example.

The system is far from perfect. Overlaps persist, and I have to be sure that with each new tale a significantly different route map must be established lest it be confused with similar features of a recent predecessor. Thus, first impressions notwithstanding, it is not prudent to associate all matters of nutrition with one room, of seduction or sex with another, of intellectual exchange with a third. Better to rely on micro-geography (this drawer follows that closet on that wall) than to trust in the logic of the conventional mental furniture on which we depend.

I am struck by the frequency with which people comment on the perceived difficulty inherent in arranging one's thoughts *spatially* in order to be able to retrieve them a few hours later. I, admittedly from within the unusual constraints of my physical imprisonment, have come to see this as the easiest of devices—almost too mechanical, inviting me as it does to arrange examples and sequences and paradoxes in tidy ways which may misleadingly reorder the original and far more suggestive confusion of impressions and recollections.

I wonder whether it doesn't help to be male: the conventional sort of male who is on the average better at parking cars and recalling spatial arrangements than the conventional kind of woman who does better on tests requiring recollection of persons and impressions? As a child I had a bit of a party piece which consisted of map-reading a car through a strange city whose configurations I had only ever studied once, and that briefly. Conversely, I was and remain useless at the first requirement of the ambitious politician: the capacity to navigate a dinner party, recalling the domestic arrangements and political prejudices of all present before bidding them farewell by first name. There must be a mnemonic device for this too, but I have never chanced upon it.

At the time of writing (May 2010) I have completed since the onset of my disease a small political book, a public lecture, some twenty *feuilletons* reflecting on my life, and a considerable body of interviews directed towards a full-scale study of the twentieth century. All of these rest on little more than nocturnal visits to my memory chalet and subsequent efforts to recapture in sequence and in detail the content of those visits. Some look inward—beginning with a house or a bus or a man; others look out, spanning decades of political observation and engagement and continents of travel, teaching, and commentary.

To be sure, there have been nights when I have sat, comfortably enough, across from Rachel Roberts or just an empty space: people and places have wandered in only to wander out again. On such unproductive occasions I don't linger very long. I retreat to the old wooden front door, step through it onto the mountainside of the Bernese Oberland— bending geography to the will of childish association—and sit, somewhat grumpily, on a bench. Here, transformed from Rachel Roberts's guiltily entranced little auditor into Heidi's introverted alm-uncle, I pass the hours from wakeful sleep through somnolent consciousness—before awakening to the irritated awareness that I have managed to create, store, and recall precisely nothing from my previous night's efforts.

Underproductive nights are almost physically frustrating. To be sure, you can say to yourself, come now: you should be proud of the fact that you have kept your sanity—where is it written that you should be productive in addition? And yet, I feel a certain guilt at having submitted to fate so readily. Who could do any better in the circumstances? The answer, of course, is "a better me" and it is surprising how often we ask that we be a better version of our present self—in the full knowledge of just how difficult it was getting this far.

I don't resent this particular trick that conscience plays on us. But it opens up the night to the risks of the dark side; these should not be underestimated. The alm-uncle, glowering from beneath his furrowed brow at all comers, is not a happy man: his gloom only occasionally dispersed by nights spent stocking closets and drawers, shelves and corridors with the byproducts of retrieved memory.

Note that the alm-uncle, my perennially dissatisfied alter ego, does not just sit at the door of a chalet frustrated of purpose. He sits there smoking a Gitanes, cradling a glass of whisky, turning the pages of a newspaper, stomping idly across the snow-strewn streets, whistling nostalgically—and generally comporting himself as a free man. There are nights when this is all he can manage. An embittered reminder of loss? Or just the consolation of the remembered cigarette.

But other nights I walk right past him: everything

works. The faces return, the examples fit, the sepia photographs come back to life, "all connects" and within a few minutes I have my story, my characters, illustrations, and morale. The alm-uncle and his dyspeptic reminders of the world I have lost weigh as nothing: the past surrounds me and I have what I need.

But which past? The little histories that take shape in my head as I lie sheathed in nocturnal gloom are unlike anything I have written before. Even by the ultra-rational demands of my profession I was always a "reasoner": of all the clichés about "History," the one that most appealed to me was the assertion that we are but philosophers teaching with examples. I still believe this is true, though I now find myself doing it by a distinctly indirect route.

In earlier days I might have envisaged myself as a literary Gepetto, building little Pinocchios of assertion and evidence, given life by the plausibility of their logical construction and telling the truth by virtue of the necessary honesty of their separate parts. But my latest writings have a far more *inductive* quality to them. Their value rests on an essentially impressionistic effect: the success with which I have related and interwoven the private and the public, the reasoned and the intuited, the recalled and the felt.

I don't know what sort of a genre this is. Certainly the resulting little wooden boys seem to me both more loosely articulated and yet more fully human than their deductively constructed, rigorously predesigned forebears. In more polemical form—"Austerity," perhaps—they seem to me unintentionally to recall the long-forgotten *feuilletons* of Karl Kraus's Vienna: allusive, suggestive, almost too light for their urgent content. But others—in a more affectionate vein, recalling "Food" or perhaps "Putney"—serve the contrary purpose. By avoiding the heavy abstractions so familiar from the prose of "identity-seeking" narrators, they may succeed in discovering precisely such buried contours without claiming to do so.

Reading over these *feuilletons* I suppose I am struck by the man I never became. Many decades ago I was advised to study literature; history, it was suggested to me by a wise schoolmaster, would play too readily towards the grain of my instincts—allowing me to do what came easiest. Literature— poetry in particular—would force me to find within myself unfamiliar words and styles to which I might yet discover a certain affinity. I can hardly say that I regret not following this advice: my conservative intellectual habits have served me well enough. But I do think something was lost.

Thus I realize that as a child I was observing far more than I understood. Perhaps all children do this, in which case what distinguishes me is only the opportunity that catastrophic ill health has afforded me to retrieve those observations in a consistent manner. And yet I wonder. When people ask me "But how do you remember the *smell* of the

Green Line bus?" or "What was it about the detail of French country hotels that so stuck with you?" the implication is that some sort of little memory chalets were already under construction.

But nothing could be further from the truth. I just lived that childish past, perhaps connecting it up to other bits of itself more than most children are wont to do, but certainly never imaginatively repositioning it in my memory for future use. To be sure, I was a solitary child and kept my thoughts to myself. But this hardly renders me distinctive. If memory came back to me so readily in recent months, I think it is for a different reason.

The advantage of my profession is that you have a story into which you can insert example, detail, illustration. As a historian of the postwar world, recalling in silent self-interrogation details of his own life as lived through it, I have the advantage of a narrative which both connects and embellishes otherwise disjointed recollections. To be blunt, what distinguishes me from many others who—as my recent correspondence suggests—have comparable memories is that I have a variety of uses to which I can put them. For this alone I consider myself a very lucky man.

It might be thought the height of poor taste to ascribe good fortune to a healthy man with a young family struck down at the age of sixty by an incurable degenerative disorder from which he must shortly die. But there is more than one sort of luck. To fall prey to a motor neuron disease is surely to have offended the Gods at some point, and there is nothing more to be said. But if you must suffer thus, better to have a well-stocked head: full of recyclable and multi-purpose pieces of serviceable recollection, readily available to an analytically disposed mind. All that was missing was a storage cupboard. That I should have been fortunate enough to find this too among the trawlings of a lifetime seems to me close to good fortune. I hope I have put it to some use.

Tony Judt
New York,
May 2010

II

Night

I suffer from a motor neuron disorder, in my case a variant of amyotrophic lateral sclerosis (ALS): Lou Gehrig's disease. Motor neuron disorders are far from rare: Parkinson's disease, multiple sclerosis, and a variety of lesser diseases all come under that heading. What is distinctive about ALS—the least common of this family of neuro-muscular illnesses—is firstly that there is no loss of sensation (a mixed blessing) and secondly that there is no pain. In contrast to almost every other serious or deadly disease, one is thus left free to contemplate at leisure and in minimal discomfort the catastrophic progress of one's own deterioration.

In effect, ALS constitutes progressive imprisonment without parole. First you lose the use of a digit or two; then a limb; then and almost inevitably, all four. The muscles of the torso decline into near torpor, a practical problem from the digestive point of view but also life-threatening, in that breathing becomes at first difficult and eventually impossible without external assistance in the form of a tube-and-pump apparatus. In the more extreme variants of the disease, associated with dysfunction of the upper motor neurons (the rest of the body is driven by the so-called lower motor neurons), swallowing, speaking, and even controlling the jaw and head become impossible. I do not (yet) suffer from this aspect of the disease, or else I could not dictate this text.

By my present stage of decline, I am thus effectively quadriplegic. With extraordinary effort I can move my right hand a little and can adduct my left arm some six inches across my chest. My legs, although they will lock when upright long enough to allow a nurse to transfer me from one chair to another, cannot bear my weight and only one of them has any autonomous movement left in it. Thus when legs or arms are set in a given position, there they remain until someone moves them for me. The same is true of my torso, with the result that backache from inertia and pressure is a chronic irritation. Having no use of my arms, I cannot scratch an itch, adjust my spectacles, remove food particles from my teeth, or anything else that—as a moment's reflection will confirm—we all do dozens of times a day. To say the least, I am utterly and completely dependent upon the kindness of strangers (and anyone else).

During the day I can at least request a scratch, an ad-

justment, a drink, or simply a gratuitous re-placement of my
limbs—since enforced stillness for hours on end is not only
physically uncomfortable but psychologically close to intolerable. It is not as though you lose the desire to stretch, to
bend, to stand or lie or run or even exercise. But when the
urge comes over you there is nothing—nothing—that you
can do except seek some tiny substitute or else find a way to
suppress the thought and the accompanying muscle memory.

But then comes the night. I leave bedtime until the last
possible moment compatible with my nurse's need for sleep.
Once I have been "prepared" for bed I am rolled into the
bedroom in the wheelchair where I have spent the past eighteen hours. With some difficulty (despite my reduced height,
mass, and bulk I am still a substantial dead weight for even a
strong man to shift) I am maneuvered onto my cot. I am sat
upright at an angle of some 110° and wedged into place with
folded towels and pillows, my left leg in particular turned out
ballet-like to compensate for its propensity to collapse inward. This process requires considerable concentration. If I
allow a stray limb to be mis-placed, or fail to insist on having
my midriff carefully aligned with legs and head, I shall suffer
the agonies of the damned later in the night.

I am then covered, my hands placed outside the blanket
to afford me the illusion of mobility but wrapped nonetheless
since—like the rest of me—they now suffer from a permanent sensation of cold. I am offered a final scratch on any of
a dozen itchy spots from hairline to toe; the Bi-Pap breathing

device in my nose is adjusted to a necessarily uncomfortable level of tightness to ensure that it does not slip in the night; my glasses are removed . . . and there I lie: trussed, myopic, and motionless like a modern-day mummy, alone in my corporeal prison, accompanied for the rest of the night only by my thoughts.

Of course, I do have access to help if I need it. Since I can't move a muscle, save only my neck and head, my communication device is a baby's intercom at my bedside, left permanently on so that a mere call from me will bring assistance. In the early stages of my disease the temptation to call out for help was almost irresistible: every muscle felt in need of movement, every inch of skin itched, my bladder found mysterious ways to refill itself in the night and thus require relief, and in general I felt a desperate need for the reassurance of light, company, and the simple comforts of human intercourse. By now, however, I have learned to forgo this most nights, finding solace and recourse in my own thoughts.

The latter, though I say it myself, is no small undertaking. Ask yourself how often you move in the night. I don't mean change location altogether (e.g., to go to the bathroom, though that too): merely how often you shift a hand, a foot; how frequently you scratch assorted body parts before dropping off; how unselfconsciously you alter position very slightly to find the most comfortable one. Imagine for a moment that you had been obliged instead to lie absolutely motionless on your back—by no means the best sleeping position, but the only one I can tolerate—for seven unbroken hours and constrained to come up with ways to render this Calvary tolerable not just for one night but for the rest of your life.

My solution has been to scroll through my life, my thoughts, my fantasies, my memories, mis-memories, and the like until I have chanced upon events, people, or narratives that I can employ to divert my mind from the body in which it is encased. These mental exercises have to be interesting enough to hold my attention and see me through an intolerable itch in my inner ear or lower back; but they also have to be boring and predictable enough to serve as a reliable prelude and encouragement to sleep. It took me some time to identify this process as a workable alternative to insomnia and physical discomfort and it is by no means infallible. But I am occasionally astonished, when I reflect upon the matter, at how readily I seem to get through, night after night, week after week, month after month, what was once an almost insufferable nocturnal ordeal. I wake up in exactly the position, frame of mind, and state of suspended despair with which I went to bed—which in the circumstances might be thought a considerable achievement.

This cockroach-like existence is cumulatively intolerable even though on any given night it is perfectly manageable. "Cockroach" is of course an allusion to Kafka's *Metamorphosis*, in which the protagonist wakes up one morning to discover that he has been transformed into an insect. The point of the story is as much the responses and incomprehension of his family as it is the account of his own sensations, and it is hard to resist the thought that even the best-meaning and most generously thoughtful friend or relative cannot hope to understand the sense of isolation and imprisonment that this disease imposes upon its victims. Helplessness is humiliating even in a passing crisis—imagine or recall some occasion when you have fallen down or otherwise required physical assistance from strangers. Imagine the mind's response to the knowledge that the peculiarly humiliating helplessness of ALS is a life sentence (we speak blithely of death sentences in this connection, but actually the latter would be a relief).

Morning brings some respite, though it says something about the lonely journey through the night that the prospect of being transferred to a wheelchair for the rest of the day should raise one's spirits! Having something to do, in my case something purely cerebral and verbal, is a salutary diversion— if only in the almost literal sense of providing an occasion to communicate with the outside world and express in words, often angry words, the bottled-up irritations and frustrations of physical inanition.

The best way to survive the night would be to treat it like the day. If I could find people who had nothing better to do than talk to me all night about something sufficiently diverting to keep us both awake, I would search them out. But one is also and always aware in this disease of the necessary *normalcy* of other people's lives: their need for exercise, en-

tertainment, and sleep. And so my nights superficially resemble those of other people. I prepare for bed; I go to bed; I
get up (or, rather, am got up). But the bit between is, like the
disease itself, incommunicable.

I suppose I should be at least mildly satisfied to know
that I have found within myself the sort of survival mecha-
nism that most normal people only read about in accounts of
natural disasters or isolation cells. And it is true that this disease has its enabling dimension: thanks to my inability to take
notes or prepare them, my memory—already quite good—
has improved considerably, with the help of techniques
adapted from the "memory palace" so intriguingly depicted
by Jonathan Spence. But the satisfactions of compensation
are notoriously fleeting. There is no saving grace in being
confined to an iron suit, cold and unforgiving. The pleasures
of mental agility are much overstated, inevitably—as it now
appears to me—by those not exclusively dependent upon
them. Much the same can be said of well-meaning encourage-
ments to find nonphysical compensations for physical inad-
equacy. That way lies futility. Loss is loss, and nothing is
gained by calling it by a nicer name. My nights are intriguing;
but I could do without them.

PART ONE

III

Austerity

My wife earnestly instructs Chinese restaurants to deliver in cardboard cartons. My children are depressingly knowledgeable about climate change. Ours is an environmental family: by their standards, I am a prelapsarian relic from the age of ecological innocence. But who traipses through the apartment switching off lights and checking for leaking faucets? Who favors make-do-and-mend in an era of instant replacement? Who recycles leftovers and carefully preserves old wrapping paper? My sons nudge their friends: Dad grew up in poverty. Not at all, I correct them: I grew up in austerity.

After the war everything was in short supply. Churchill had mortgaged Great Britain and bankrupted the Treasury in order to defeat Hitler. Clothes were rationed until 1949, cheap and simple "utility furniture" until 1952, food until 1954. The rules were briefly suspended for the coronation of Elizabeth, in June 1953: everyone was allowed one extra pound of sugar and four ounces of margarine. But this exercise in supererogatory generosity served only to underscore the dreary regime of daily life.

To a child, rationing was part of the natural order. Indeed, long after the practice ceased, my mother convinced me that "sweets" (candy) were still restricted. When I protested that school friends appeared to have unlimited access to the stuff, she explained disapprovingly that their parents must be on the black market. Her story was all the more credible because the legacy of war was ever-present. London was pockmarked with bomb sites: where once there had been houses, streets, railway yards, or warehouses there were now large roped-off areas of dirt, usually with a dip in the middle where the bomb had fallen. By the early 1950s unexploded ordnance had been mostly cleared and bomb sites—though off-limits—were no longer dangerous. But these impromptu play spaces were irresistible for small boys.

Rationing and subsidies meant that the bare necessities of life were accessible to all. Courtesy of the postwar Labour government, children were entitled to a range of healthful products: free milk but also concentrated orange juice and cod-liver oil—obtainable only in pharmacies after you established your identity. The orange juice came in rectangular, medicine-like glass bottles and I have never quite lost the association. Even today, a large glassful prompts in me a sub-limated pang of guilt: better not drink it all at once. Of cod-liver oil, urged upon housewives and mothers by benevolently intrusive authorities, the less said the better.

We were fortunate to lease an apartment above the hair-dressing shop where my parents worked, but many of my friends lived in substandard or temporary housing. Every British government from 1945 through the mid-1960s com-mitted itself to large-scale public housing schemes: all fell short. In the early 1950s, thousands of Londoners still lived in "prefabs": urban trailer parks for the homeless, ostensibly temporary but often lasting for years.

Postwar guidelines for new housing were minimalist: three-bedroom houses were to comprise at least nine hun-dred square feet of living space—about the size of a spacious one-bedroom apartment in contemporary Manhattan. Look-ing back, these homes seem not merely pokey, but chilly and underfurnished. At the time, there were long waiting lists: owned and managed by local authorities, such houses were intensely desirable.

The air over the capital resembled a bad day in Beijing; coal was the fuel of choice—cheap, abundant, and domesti-cally produced. Smog was a perennial hazard: I recall leaning out of the car window, my face enveloped in a dense yellow haze, instructing my father on his distance from the curb—you could literally not see beyond an arm's length ahead of you and the smell was awful. But everyone "muddled through together": Dunkirk and the Blitz were freely invoked without a hint of irony to illustrate a sense of national grit and Londoners' capacity to "take it"—first Hitler, now this.

I grew up at least as familiar with World War I as with the one that had just ended. Veterans, memorials, and invocations abounded; but the ostentatious patriotism of contemporary American bellicosity was altogether absent. War, too, was austere: I had two uncles who fought with Montgomery's Eighth Army from Africa through Italy and there was nothing nostalgic or triumphalist in their accounts of shortage, error, and incompetence. Arrogant music hall evocations of empire—

We don't want to fight them, but by Jingo if we do,
We've got the ships, we've got the men,
we've got the money too!

—had been replaced by the wartime radio lament of Vera Lynn: *We'll meet again, don't know where, don't know when.* Even in the afterglow of victory, things would never be the same.

Reiterated references to the recent past established a bridge between my parents' generation and my own. The world of the 1930s was with us still: George Orwell's *Road to Wigan Pier*, J.B. Priestley's *Angel Pavement*, and Arnold

Bennett's *The Grim Smile of the Five Towns* all spoke to an England very much present. Wherever you looked, there were affectionate allusions to imperial glory—India was "lost" a few months after I was born. Biscuit tins, pencil holders, schoolbooks, and cinema newsreels reminded us of who we were and what we had achieved. "We" is no mere grammatical convention: when Humphrey Jennings produced a documentary to celebrate the 1951 Festival of Britain, he called it *Family Portrait*. The family might have fallen on hard times, but we were all in it together.

It was this "togetherness" that made tolerable the characteristic shortages and grayness of postwar Britain. Of course, we weren't *really* a family: if we were, then the wrong members—as Orwell had once noted—were still in charge. All the same, since the war the rich kept a prudently low profile. There was little evidence in those years of conspicuous consumption. Everyone looked the same and dressed in the same materials: worsted, flannel, or corduroy. People came in modest colors—brown, beige, gray—and lived remarkably similar lives. We schoolchildren accepted uniforms all the more readily because our parents too appeared in sartorial lockstep. In April 1947, the ever-dyspeptic Cyril Connolly wrote of our "drab clothes, our ration books and murder stories. . . . London [is] now the largest, saddest and dirtiest of great cities."

Great Britain would eventually emerge from postwar penury—though with less panache and self-confidence than its European neighbors. For anyone whose memories go back no further than the later 1950s, "austerity" is an abstraction. Rationing and restrictions were gone, housing was available: the characteristic bleakness of postwar Britain was lifting. Even the smog was abating, now that coal had been replaced by electricity and cheap fuel oil.

Curiously, the escapist British cinema of the immediate postwar years—*Spring in Park Lane* (1948) or *Maytime in Mayfair* (1949), with Michael Wilding and Anna Neagle— had been replaced by hard-boiled "kitchen sink" dramas starring working-class lads played by Albert Finney or Alan Bates in gritty industrial settings: *Saturday Night and Sunday Morning* (1960) or *A Kind of Loving* (1962). But these films were set in the north, where austerity lingered. Watching them in London was like seeing one's childhood played back across a time warp: in the south, by 1957, the Conservative Prime Minister Harold Macmillan could assure his listeners that most of them had "never had it so good." He was right.

I don't think I fully appreciated the impact of those early childhood years until quite recently. Looking back from our present vantage point, one sees more clearly the virtues of that bare-bones age. No one would welcome its return. But austerity was not just an economic condition: it aspired to a public ethic. Clement Attlee, the Labour prime minister from 1945 to 1951, had emerged—like Harry

Truman—from the shadow of a charismatic war leader and embodied the reduced expectations of the age.

Churchill mockingly described him as a modest man "who has much to be modest about." But it was Attlee who presided over the greatest age of reform in modern British history—comparable to the achievements of Lyndon Johnson two decades later but under far less auspicious circumstances. Like Truman, he lived and died parsimoniously—reaping scant material gain from a lifetime of public service. Attlee was an exemplary representative of the great age of middle-class Edwardian reformers: morally serious and a trifle austere. Who among our present leaders could make such a claim—or even understand it?

Moral seriousness in public life is like pornography: hard to define but you know it when you see it. It describes a coherence of intention and action, an ethic of political responsibility. All politics is the art of the possible. But art too has its ethic. If politicians were painters, with FDR as Titian and Churchill as Rubens, then Attlee would be the Vermeer of the profession: precise, restrained—and long undervalued. Bill Clinton might aspire to the heights of Salvador Dalí (and believe himself complimented by the comparison), Tony Blair to the standing—and cupidity—of Damien Hirst.

In the arts, moral seriousness speaks to an economy of form and aesthetic restraint: the world of *The Bicycle Thief*. I recently introduced our twelve-year-old son to François Truffaut's 1959 classic *Les Quatre Cents Coups* (*The 400 Blows*). Of a generation raised on a diet of contemporary "message" cinema from *The Day After Tomorrow* through *Avatar*, he was stunned: "It's spare. He does so much with so little." Quite so. The wealth of resources we apply to entertainment serves only to shield us from the poverty of the product; likewise in politics, where ceaseless chatter and grandiloquent rhetoric mask a yawning emptiness.

The opposite of austerity is not prosperity but *luxe et volupté*. We have substituted endless commerce for public purpose, and expect no higher aspirations from our leaders. Sixty years after Churchill could offer only "blood, toil, tears and sweat," our very own war president—notwithstanding the hyperventilated moralism of his rhetoric—could think of nothing more to ask of us in the wake of September 11, 2001, than to continue shopping. This impoverished view of community—the "togetherness" of consumption—is all we deserve from those who now govern us. If we want better rulers, we must learn to ask more from them and less for ourselves. A little austerity might be in order.

IV

Food

Just because you grow up on bad food, it does not follow that you lack nostalgia for it. My own gastronomic youth was firmly bounded by everything that was least inspiring in traditional English cuisine, alleviated with hints of Continental cosmopolitanism occasionally introduced by my father's fading memories of a Belgian youth, and interspersed with weekly reminders of another heritage altogether: Sabbath evening dinners at the home of my East European Jewish grandparents. This curious mélange did little to sharpen my taste buds—it was not until I lived in France as a graduate student that I encountered good food on a regular basis—but it added further to the confusions of my youthful identity.

My mother was born in the least Jewish part of the old

London East End: at the intersection of Burdett Road and the Commercial Road, a few blocks north of the London Docks. This topographical misfortune—she always felt a little tangential to her surroundings, lacking the intensely Jewish milieu of Stepney Green a few hundred yards to the north—played into many otherwise curious aspects of her personality. Unlike my father, for example, my mother had great respect for the King and the Queen, and was always half-tempted to stand up during the Queen's speech on television in later years. She was discreet to the point of embarrassment about her Jewishness, in contrast to the overtly foreign and Yiddish quality of most of the rest of our extended family. And in an inverted tribute to her own mother's indifference to Jewish traditions beyond those ordained by annual rituals (and the decidedly Cockney ambiance of the streets where she grew up), she had almost no knowledge of Jewish cuisine.

As a result, I was brought up on English food. But not fish and chips, spotted dick, toad in the hole, Yorkshire pud, or other delicacies of British home cooking. These my mother scorned as somehow unhealthy; she may have grown up surrounded by non-Jews, but for just that reason she and her family kept to themselves and knew little of the domestic world of their neighbors, which they looked upon with fear and suspicion. In any case, she had no idea how to prepare "English delicacies." Her occasional encounters, via my father's friends in the Socialist Party of Great Britain, with vegetarians and vegans had taught her the virtues of brown bread, brown rice, green beans, and other "healthy" staples of an Edwardian left-wing diet. But she could no more cook brown rice than she could have prepared "chop suey." And so she did what every other cook in England in those days did: she boiled everything to death.

It was thus that I came to associate English food not so much with the absence of subtlety as with the absence of any flavor whatsoever. We had Hovis brown bread, which always seemed to me even more boring in its worthy way than the rubberized white toast served for tea at my friends' houses. We ate boiled meat, boiled greens, and, very occasionally, fried versions of same (to be fair, fish my mother could indeed fry with some style—though whether this was an English or a Jewish attribute I never could tell). Cheese, when it appeared, was usually Dutch—for reasons that I never understood. Tea was ubiquitous. My parents disapproved of fizzy drinks—another unfortunate heritage of their political dalliances—so we drank fruitified, uncarbonated soft drinks, or Nescafé in later years. Thanks to my father, Camembert, salad, real coffee, and other treats occasionally surfaced. But my mother regarded these with much the same suspicion she harbored towards other Continental imports, gastronomic and human alike.

The contrast with the food that my paternal grandmother prepared for us every Friday night at her house in North London could thus not have been greater. My grandfather was Polish-Jewish, my grandmother born in a Lithuanian shtetl. Their taste in food ran to Northeast European Jewish. It was not until decades later that I was to taste the flavors, variety, and texture of the Jewish cuisine of South-Central Europe (Hungary, in particular), nor did I have the slightest familiarity with the Mediterranean cooking of the Sephardic tradition. My grandmother, who had made her way from Pilvistok to London via Antwerp, knew nothing of salad and she had never met a green vegetable she could not torture to death in a saucepan. But with sauces, chicken, fish, beef, root vegetables, and fruit she was—to my understimulated palate—a magician.

The characteristic quality of a Friday night dinner in those days was the repeated contrast between soft and crunchy, sweet and savory. Potatoes, swedes, turnips were always brown and soft and appeared to have been drenched in sugar. Cucumbers, onions, and other small, harmless vegetables came crunchy and pickled. Meat fell off the fork, having long since fallen off the bone. It too was brown and soft. Fish—gefilted, boiled, pickled, fried, or smoked—was omnipresent and the house seemed to me always to smell of spiced and preserved sea creatures. Interestingly and perhaps revealingly, I have no recollection of the texture of the fish or of its provenance (probably carp). It was its wrapping that one noticed.

Along with the fish and the vegetables there came dessert. Or, more precisely, "compote." All manner of stewed and squeezed fruits, prominent among them plums and pears, would appear faithfully after the main course. Occasionally they had been compressed inside a thick pastry of the kind traditionally employed in Purim hamantaschen, but more commonly the compote was freestanding. Liquid refreshment consisted always and uniquely of a horrible sweet wine for the adults and lemon tea for everyone. Together with bulk in the form of black bread, challah, matzoh balls in soup, and dumplings in all shapes and varieties (but only one texture— soft), this meal would have been recognizable to anyone born between Germany and Russia, Latvia and Romania in the course of the past half-millennium. For me, transported weekly from Putney to Pilvistok, it represented Family, Familiarity, Flavor, and Roots. I never even attempted to explain to my English schoolboy friends what we ate on Friday nights or what it meant to me. I don't think I knew and they would never have understood.

As I grew older, I discovered other ways to add taste to a hopelessly, helplessly bland domestic regimen. In England in those days there were just three paths to interesting food if your grandparents did not happen to come from exotic foreign parts. There was Italian food, still confined to Soho and the bohemian fringes of the aspirant talking classes. This was beyond my teenage or student budget. Then there was Chinese food, not particularly interesting or widely available in those years and in any case commercially adapted to British taste. The only serious Chinese restaurants in London before the mid-Sixties were in the East End and patronized by Chinese sailors and a handful of East Asian immigrants. The menus were frequently untranslated and the dishes unknown to locals.

The real escape route lay to the Indies. I don't believe my parents ever went to an Indian restaurant—my mother was under the curious illusion that whereas Chinese food (about which she knew nothing) was somehow "clean," Indian food was suspiciously camouflaged in flavor and probably cooked on the floor. I never shared this prejudice and spent most of my student years and disposable income in Indian restaurants in London and Cambridge. At the time I just thought it delectable, but on reflection it is likely that I made an unconscious association with my grandparents' table.

Indian food too consisted of overcooked protein drenched in flavorful sauces. Its bread was soft, its condiments spicy, its vegetables sweet. In place of dessert came fruit-flavored ices or exotic fruit compotes. And it was best accompanied by beer, a beverage hardly known in our home. My father never vouchsafed the thought, but I'm sure that somewhere deep inside him resided a prejudice against pub-crawling, beer-swilling ethnic Englishmen. He was European enough to drink decent wine, but otherwise shared the older Jewish prejudice against excess alcohol consumption.

Indian food made me more English. Like most Englishmen of my generation I now think of takeout or delivered Indian food as a native dish imported centuries before. I am English enough to think of Indian food in particular as an aspect of England that I miss here in the US where Chinese is the ethnic dish of local preference. But my Englishness also leads me to miss East European Jewish cuisine in its very slightly adapted British form (a little more boiling, a little less spice than Jewish cooking here in the US). I can work up a nostalgia for fish and chips, but in truth it is nothing more than a self generated gastronomic Heritage Exercise. We hardly ever ate the stuff when I was a child. Were I ever truly to set out in Search of Past Taste I would begin with braised beef and baked turnip, followed by chicken tikka masala and pickled wollies swabbed in challah, Kingfisher beer and sweet lemon tea. As for the madeleine that would trigger the memory? Naan dunked in matzoh ball soup, served by a Yiddish-speaking waiter from Madras. We are what we ate. And I am very English.

V

Cars

According to my mother, my father was "obsessed" with motor cars. In her view, the perennial fragility of our domestic economy was owed to her husband's proclivity to spend all our spare cash on them. I cannot judge whether she was right about this—it's pretty clear that, left to her own devices, she would have confined the family to one small car per decade, if at all—but even to the sympathetic eyes of his admiring son my father did appear somewhat absorbed in his cars; and particularly in Citroëns, the French company whose idiosyncratic products graced our front yard throughout my childhood and adolescence. There was the occasional soon-to-be-regretted English impulse purchase—a convertible Austin A40, a sporty AC Ace—and a rather more enduring fling with a DB Panhard, of which more below; but year in, year out Joe Judt drove, talked and fixed Citroëns.

That my father should have been so besotted with the internal combustion engine was thoroughly in keeping with his generation. The "car culture" came to Western Europe in the 1950s, which is about the point at which my father was in a position to join it. Men born before World War I were well into middle age before cars were available to most Europeans: in the '30s and '40s they were confined to pokey little runabouts notorious for their discomfort and unreliability and could not afford anything better until well past their prime. My generation, by contrast, grew up with cars and saw nothing distinctively appealing or romantic about them. But for men—and, I suppose, a handful of women—born between the wars, the motor car symbolized a newfound freedom and prosperity. They could afford one and there were many available. Petrol was cheap and the roads still appealingly empty.

I never fully understood why we had to drive a Citroën. My father's ideological position on the matter was that Citroëns were the most technologically advanced cars on the road: in 1936, when the company first manufactured its Traction Avant, with front-wheel drive and independent suspension, this was certainly true—as it became once again in 1956 with the unveiling of the sexily aerodynamic DS19. The cars were unquestionably more comfortable than most comparable family saloons, and probably safer. Whether they were more reliable is another matter: in the days before the Japanese automobile revolution no road cars were particularly reliable and I spent many tedious evenings handing tools to my father as he tinkered with some dysfunctional engine part late into the night.

In retrospect, I wonder whether my father's insistence upon buying Citroëns—of which we must have owned at least eight in the course of my childhood—had something to do with his early life. He was, after all, an immigrant—born in Belgium, raised there and in Ireland—who only arrived in England in 1935. In time he learned to speak impeccable English, but underneath he remained a continental: his taste for salads, cheeses, coffee, and wine ran frequently afoul of my mother's characteristically English unconcern for food and drink except as a fueling resource. And thus, just as my father resented Nescafé and preferred Camembert, so he disdained Morrises, Austins, Standard Vanguards, and other generic English products, looking instinctively to the Continent instead.

As to why we should have become a "Citroën" family, when Volkswagens, Peugeots, Renaults, Fiats, and the rest were all readily available and cheaper, I like to think that there was some subliminal ethnic motive at work. German cars were of course out of the question. The reputation of Italian cars (at any rate those we could afford) was at its lowest point: Italians, it was widely felt, could design anything— they just couldn't build it. Renault was disgraced by its founder's active collaboration with the Nazis (as a result of which the firm had been nationalized). Peugeot was a re-spectable outfit but better known in those years for their bikes; their cars, in any case, were built like tanks and seemed to lack pizzazz (the same argument was made against Volvos). And, perhaps the decisive if undeclared consideration, the eponymous founder of the Citroën dynasty had been a Jew.

There was something slightly embarrassing about our cars. They suggested, in an age of austerity and provincialism, an aggressively exotic and "foreign" quality to the family—causing my mother in particular to feel uneasy. And of course they were (relatively) expensive and thus ostentatious. I recall one occasion in the mid-fifties when we drove across London to visit my maternal grandparents, who lived in a run-down terraced house on a side street in Bow. Cars in that part of London were still thin on the ground and were most likely to be little black Ford Populars and Morris Minors, testaments to the limited means and conventional tastes of their owners. And here we were, clambering out of a shining white Citroën DS19, like aristocrats come to inspect their lowly tenants. I don't know how my mother felt—I never asked. My father was enjoyably absorbed in the envious attention his new car was attracting. I wanted to disappear down the nearest manhole.

For a few years around 1960, my father's obsession with cars took him into amateur motor sport. Every Sunday the two of us would trawl north to Norfolk or the East Midlands, where fellow enthusiasts mounted scheduled programs of car racing. My father's vehicle was a tuned-up Panhard DB, a pretty little car which made seductive noises and competed reasonably effectively against the Triumph Spitfires and MGBs of the age. Assorted family friends were inveigled (for remuneration? I never knew) into serving as "mechanics" while I was assigned the curiously responsible job of setting the tire pressures before the race. This was fun in its way, though the atmospherics could get tedious (grown men discussing carburetors for hours at a time) and the round-trip journeys took up to six hours.

Far more entertaining were the continental holidays which we took in those years: largely, it sometimes felt, in order to give my father an excuse for a long drive. In those pre-*autoroute* years a continental road trip was an adventure: everything took a long time and something always broke down. Sitting on the "wrong" side of the front seat, I had a driver's eye view of France's glorious *routes nationales*. I was also the first to be accosted by policemen whenever we were stopped for speeding or, on one memorable occasion deep in the night somewhere outside Paris, caught in a military "sweep" during the OAS crisis.

We mostly traveled as a family. My mother could not have cared less whether she spent her holidays in Brighton or Biarritz, and she found long road trips tedious and tiring. But in those days families did things together and part of the point of a car was to go on "outings." For me, at least (and in this respect I probably resembled my father), the object of the exercise was the journey—the places we went to, especially on Sunday "jaunts," were often conventional and of scant redeeming interest. Even across the Channel, the best part of our summer and winter holidays was always the adventure entailed in getting there: the punctures, the icy roads, the dangerous business of overtaking on narrow winding country lanes, the exotic little hotels reached late in the night after long hours of embittered domestic squabbling over when and where to halt. It was in the car that my father was most at home and my mother least so. Considering the amount of time we spent on the road in those years, it is remarkable that their marriage lasted even as long as it did.

Looking back, I am perhaps more sympathetic to my father's self-indulgence than I was at the time, for all the pleasure I took in our family travels. I see him now as a frustrated man: trapped in an unhappy marriage and doing work which bored and perhaps even humiliated him. Cars—cars to race, cars to discuss, cars to tinker with, and cars to take him home to Europe—were his community. Not caring much for pubs or drink, and with no workmates, he turned the Citroën car into an all-purpose companion and visiting card—culminating in his election to the presidency of the Citroën Car Club of Great Britain. What other men sought and found in alcohol and mistresses, my father sublimated into his love affair with a car company—which no doubt accounts for my mother's instinctive hostility to the whole business.

Upon turning seventeen I dutifully learned to drive and in due course acquired the first of many cars: inevitably, a Citroën, a cheap little 2CV. But although I enjoyed the experience and was eventually to transport assorted girlfriends and wives across much of Europe and the continental US, driving never meant to me what it meant to my father. Finding little charm in cold country garages and lacking the requisite technical skills myself, I soon abandoned Citroëns for more reliable if less exotic brands: Hondas, Peugeots, and, eventually, a Saab. To be sure, I too indulged testosterone-driven whims: a convertible red MG celebrated my first divorce and I retain fond memories of an open Ford Mustang cruising down California's coastal Route 1. But these were always just cars, never a "culture."

This too seems to me a conventional generational response. We baby-boomers grew up with cars, as well as with fathers who adored and indulged in them. The roads onto which we graduated were more crowded, less "open" than those of the interwar and immediate postwar decades. There was little adventure to be had in driving them and not much to be discovered unless one struck out well beyond the conventional objectives. The towns we lived in were becoming hostile to the very cars they had so myopically welcomed a few years before: in New York and Paris, as in London and many other cities, it makes little sense to keep a private vehicle. The car, at the height of its hegemony, stood for individualism, liberty, privacy, separation, and selfishness in their most socially dysfunctional forms. But like many dysfunctions, it was insidiously seductive. Ozymandias-like, it now invites us to look upon its works and despair. But it was quite fun at the time.

Putney

H ome, they say, is where the heart is. I'm not so sure. I've had lots of homes and I don't consider my heart to be attached very firmly to any of them. What is meant, of course, is that home is wherever you choose to place it—in which case I suppose I've always been homeless: many decades ago I left my heart somewhere on a Swiss mountainside, but the rest of me has foolishly failed to follow. Still, among my deracinated roots there is one that protrudes a little above the heap and may even constitute a grounding of sorts. From 1952 until 1958 my family lived in the southwest London district of Putney and I recall it with affection.

I did not know it at the time, but Putney was a good address to grow up in. A hundred yards north of our flat stood St. Mary's Church, a squat, elderly parish establishment notable for the debates held there in October 1647 at the height of the English Civil War. It was here that Colonel Thomas Rainsborough famously warned his interlocutors that: "*the poorest he that is in England hath a life to live, as the greatest he . . . every man that is to live under a government ought first by his own consent to put himself under that government. . . .*" Exactly three centuries later the Labour Government of Clement Attlee would inaugurate the welfare state that was to guarantee to the poorest he (and she) a life worth living and a government that served them. Attlee was born in Putney and died only a few miles away; despite a long and successful political career he remained modest in demeanor as in wealth—in revealing contrast to his grasping, fee-gouging successors: an exemplary representative of the great age of middle-class Edwardian reformers—morally serious and a trifle austere.

In its way, there was something austere about Putney itself. It is an ancient parish—mentioned in the Domesday Book along with a ferry which crossed the Thames there (the first bridge was built in 1642)—and derives its relative importance from both the adjacent river and the old Portsmouth road that would become Putney's busy High Street. The confluence of road and river also explains why an early Underground line was routed through Putney, running north-south from Earl's Court to Wimbledon, as well as a branch of the London and Southwestern Railway (later the Southern Railway) from Windsor to Waterloo, with a station strategically pitched at the upper end of the High Street. There was an unusual affluence of buses too: the 14, 30, and 74 which ran from Putney or thereabouts to northeast London; the 22 and the 96 which started at Putney Common and traversed the City before terminating respectively in Homerton and Redbridge Station in deepest Essex (the longest bus route in London at the time); and the 85 and 93 buses which trundled south out of Putney Bridge tube station to Kingston and Morden respectively. And of course there was the 718 Green Line coach which passed through Putney on its long journey from Windsor to Harlow.

Since all eight bus and coach routes, together with two trolleybuses (electric buses powered by overhead cables, foolishly withdrawn in 1959), the Underground line and the suburban railway converged in or near the High Street, the latter was an unusually busy thoroughfare for those days. I was well-placed to appreciate this: our flat, at no. 92 Putney High Street, afforded me a privileged, if permanently noisy perch. And since I took the 14 bus to school (my Green Line adventures only began after we moved out to leafy Kingston Hill), I saw all these buses and trains up close every day. Cars were in shorter supply, but only relatively: London in those years had the greatest density of car ownership and use anywhere outside the continental United States and traffic jams were already part of Putney life.

But off the busy High Street, there was another, quieter

Putney: the established late-nineteenth-century suburb of mansion flats, subdivided Victorian terraces and Edwardian brick and stone villas, typically "semi-detached" but often quite sizeable. There were row after row, street after street, block after block of these often graceful buildings, strikingly homogenous in décor and facings. More attractive than the interminable interwar suburban sprawl of southeast London, less ostentatiously prosperous than the luxuriant, tree-lined avenues of northwest London, Putney was unmistakably and reassuringly middle class. To be sure, there were upper-middle-class enclaves, predictably located up by Putney's ancient heath and on the slopes of the hill that led to it; and there were working streets like the river-fronting Lower Richmond Road where the aspiring poet Laurie Lee found cheap lodgings and his first job after arriving in London from deepest Gloucestershire. But for the most part Putney was comfortably and securely in the middle.

Our own flat was chilly and uninspiring, rising three stories above the hairdressing shop where my parents worked. But it had the distinctive quality of backing onto Jones Mews: one of the last of the stable alleys where the residents and tradesmen of the town had kept their animals. In those years the Mews still served its traditional function: two of the six stables in the alley leading away from our back door were occupied by working animals. One of these—a bedraggled, skinny apology for a horse—slaved for a rag-and-bone man who would drag it out of its stall each morning, shove it carelessly between the shafts, and head out to collect what, by the end of the day, was often a substantial haul. The other horse fared better, working for a blowsy, chatty flower lady who had a stall on the common. The remaining stables had been converted into sheds for local artisans: electricians, mechanics, and general handymen. Like the milkman, the butcher, the flower lady, and the rag-and-bone man, these were all locals, children of locals, and beyond. From the perspective of Jones Mews, Putney was still a village.

Even the High Street was still rooted in a self-contained past. There were already, of course, "chain stores": Woolworth, Marks & Spencer, The British Home Stores, etc. But these were small outlets and far outnumbered by locally owned shops selling haberdashery, tobacco, books, groceries, shoes, ladies' wear, toiletries, and everything else. Even the "multiples" were somehow local: Sainsburys, a small store with just one double-window, still had sawdust on its floor. You were served by polite, slightly haughty assistants in starched blue-and-white aprons, resembling nothing so much as the proud employees in the photograph on the back wall showing the little shop on the day it opened many decades before. The "Home and Colonial" grocers further down the High Street carefully distinguished between its overseas and home-grown supplies: "New Zealand lamb," "English beef," and so on.

But the High Street was my mother's territory. I shopped on Lacy Road, which boasted an off-license whence I was dispatched for cider and wine; a small tailors' establishment; and two "sweet shops." One of these was generic and modern, at least by '50s standards, offering fruit gums, packaged chocolate, and Wrigley's chewing gum. But the other—darker, danker, dirtier, and otherwise depressing—was far more intriguing. It was run (and, I assume, owned) by a shriveled, mean-spirited old crone who would resentfully weigh out from an array of large glass bottles a quarter-pound of gobstoppers or liquorice while grumbling at the impatience and sartorial insufficiency of her customers: "I've been serving grubby little boys like you since the old Queen's jubilee, so don't try to fool me!" By the old Queen, of course, she meant Victoria, whose jubilee had been celebrated in Putney in June 1887. . . .

There was still something Victorian, or perhaps Edwardian would be more precise, about the feel of the side streets. Up those solid stone steps, behind the heavy window treatments, one could imagine bespectacled spinsters offering piano lessons to supplement their meager pensions—and one did not have to imagine it, since I at least was taught the instrument by two such ladies, both living in what I recognized, even then, as genteel poverty. I had school friends whose families occupied a floor or two of the imposing villas near Dover House Road or up Putney Hill, and was vaguely impressed by the sense of solidity and permanence given off by these buildings, even in their modern subdivided state.

Putney had its loose ends too. The riverbank was still

semi-rural and largely untouched—once you got past the ever-so-slightly commercialized strip near the bridge, where the annual Oxford-Cambridge Boat Race began. There were boathouses, houseboats, the occasional tug, abandoned skiffs rotting gently into the mud: living evidence of the river's ancient business. At Putney the Thames is still actively tidal: at times a narrow stream lazily bisecting great beaches of mud, at others close to overflowing its scruffy and rather under-secured banks when a ferry or pleasure boat, on its way from Westminster Bridge up to Teddington or even Oxford, sweeps under the bridge and into the great bend embracing Craven Cottage (Fulham's Football Ground) on the opposite bank. Putney's river was messy, inelegant, and functional; I spent a lot of time sitting by its edge and thinking, though I no longer remember about what.

We left Putney when I was ten years old, drawn out to the verdant Surrey fringes by my parents' brief flirtation with prosperity. The house on Kingston Hill, where we lived for nine years until my parents ran out of money, was larger than the old flat; it had a garden and a front gate. It also—oh joy!—had two toilets, a very considerable relief after the experience of no. 92 and its single water closet two icy stories down from my bedroom. And there were country lanes in Kingston for the aspirant cyclist to explore. But I never really got over Putney: its shops, its smells, its associations. There wasn't much by way of greenery, except at the edges where commons and heaths had been left as nature planted them. It was urban through and through, though urban in that informal, generous way so characteristic of London: a city that— at least until the disastrous urban "planning" of the '60s—had always grown *out* rather than *up*. I'm no longer at home there—the High Street today is no better than it ought to be, a featureless replica of every high street in England, from its fast food outlets to its mobile phone stores. But Putney was my London, and London—even though I really only lived there as a child and left forever when I went up to Cambridge in 1966—was my city. It isn't anymore. But nostalgia makes a very satisfactory second home.

VII

The Green Line Bus

For some years at the end of the Fifties, I went to school on the Green Line bus. The Green Line, publicly owned like all London buses in those days, was a division of London Transport providing long-distance bus connections across London, typically starting out in a country town twenty to thirty miles outside the city and terminating in a comparably distant town on the opposite side of London. The bus I used, the 718, was routed from Windsor in the southwest to Harlow in the northeast, halfway between London and Cambridge.

The Green Line was distinctive in a number of ways. It was green, of course, not just on the outside but in the livery and finish inside as well. The buses were typically single-decker, in contrast to the conventional London buses of the day, and they had folding electric doors that closed with a swish. This feature also distinguished them from the open-backed double-deckers of central London and gave the Green Line buses a cozy, reassuring, and rather warm feel. Because they covered such long distances for a regular bus line—the typical Green Line route entailed a trip of over three hours end to end—these buses did not stop at most of the standard bus stops but only at occasional interchange points. Despite going no faster than the average London bus, they were thus nevertheless an "express" route and could charge a little more for their services.

The color and nomenclature of this service was not fortuitous. The Green Line buses invoked and illustrated a long-standing principle of London's urban planning: their terminuses were strategically located athwart or beyond the "Green Belt" established around London in the early decades of the century. The latter constituted an early exercise in environmental preservation as well as in the provision of open space for public leisure and pleasure. The British capital in those days was thus carefully contained within a belt of open land: variously parks, common land, old-growth forests, undeveloped farmland, or open heath, all of it inherited from earlier royal or municipal or parochial property left in place so as to assure the preservation of the countryside of southeast England, perennially under threat from the unconstrained expansion of the Great Wen.

Despite the helter-skelter ribbon development of the

interwar decades, and the even less appealing public and private housing projects of the 1950s, Greater London had been more or less contained within its belt of greenery; sometimes no more than a few miles deep, but enough to distinguish the city from the country and to preserve the identity and particularity of the towns and villages on its farther side. The Green Line buses thus reflected in their name, their routes, and the distances they covered the largely successful aspirations of a generation of planners.

I, of course, knew nothing of this. But I think I instinctively grasped the implicit message of these buses and their route managers. We, they seemed to say, are the moving spirit and incarnation of a certain idea of London. We begin in Windsor, as it might be, or Stevenage, or Gravesend, or East Grinstead, and we finish up in Harlow or Guildford or Watford, straddling London as we go (most Green Line routes passed through Victoria Station, Marble Arch, or both). Whereas the red Routemasters scurry back and forth across central London, their passengers leaping on and off at will, we Greenliners box the city, acknowledging its astonishing scale but asserting, in our distinctive routes and endpoints, its necessary limits.

I sometimes essayed those limits, riding the line from one end to the other just for the sheer pleasure of seeing woods, hills, and fields emerge at each end of my native metropolis. The Green Line "team"—there was a driver and a conductor to every bus—seemed distinctly sympathetic to this ostensibly pointless childhood exercise. They were not paid much more than the drivers and conductors of the red buses—none of the employees of the London Passenger Transport Board could boast much of an income in those days. When I started using their services, the busmen had only just come off a bitter and prolonged strike. But the "mood" of the Green Line men was quite distinct. They had more time to talk to one another and to the passengers. Because their doors closed, the interior was quieter than that of other buses. And large parts of their route were so very attractive, in that settled, comfortable way of the leafy outer suburbs of postwar London, that the bus itself—despite being upholstered in much the same way as all other London buses of the day—somehow *felt* plusher and more comfortable too. And so the driver and conductor seemed to me at least to take a greater pride in their vehicle and to relax into its routine more than other busmen.

The conductor, paid a little less than the skilled driver, was usually but not always a younger man (there were hardly any women). His function was ostensibly to keep order and collect fares; but since large tracts of countryside were often covered with relatively few passengers and stops, his task was hardly preoccupying. In practice he kept the driver company. The driver in his turn was part of the bus (his compartment integrated into the interior body) and thus often well known—sometimes by his first name—to passengers on his route. There was no question of the loneliness of the long-distance driver on the Green Line buses. Whether there was a question of class is another matter. Because the Green Lines cost more and picked up passengers from the suburbs as well as across the city, many of their patrons were probably a class or so removed from the typical bus user of those days. Whereas most people who took red buses to work in the 1950s would not have been in a position to commute by car even if they had wished to, a goodly share of the Green Line business in later years was lost to automobile commuters.

Thus whereas drivers, conductors, and passengers on the inner London buses were often drawn from the same social groups, Green Line commuters were more likely to be middle-class. This probably resulted in the reproduction on the bus of some of the patterns of deference still endemic to British society at large. It also made the buses quieter. However, the rather palpable pride that the Green Line teams took in their bus—they spent more time on it and were less likely to be moved to different services at short notice, in particular the drivers who had to learn long and complicated routes—compensated in some measure for these social hierarchies. The result was that everyone on the bus felt quite pleased with themselves, or seemed to. Even at the age of eleven I remember thinking that the bus *smelled* reassuring, more like a library or an old bookstore than a means of transport. This otherwise inexplicable association probably drew on the few public places that I associated with calm rather than noise and bustle.

I continued to use the Green Line buses into the mid-Sixties. By then I was chiefly catching them late at night (the last Green Line in those days usually left its depot around 10 PM), returning from Zionist youth meetings or a tryst with a girlfriend. The Green Line at that time of the evening was usually on time (unlike the red buses it ran to a published schedule); if you were late to the stop, you missed it. In which case I would be doomed to a long and cold wait on a station platform for the rare night train, followed by a cheerless and tiring walk home from some inconveniently sited Southern Railway station. Catching the Green Line thus felt good, a comfort and a security against the chill London night and a promise of safe, warm transport home.

Today's Green Line buses are but a shadow of their predecessors. They are owned and run by Arriva, the worst of the private companies now responsible for providing train and bus services to British commuters, at exorbitant prices. With rare exceptions the buses avoid central London, being routed instead between the new reference points of British topography: Heathrow Airport, Legoland, etc. Their color is an accident of history, bearing no relation to their function: indeed, the green livery is now punctuated with pastel and other shades—an unintended reminder that neither the buses nor the service they provide stand for any integrated or common purpose. The conductors are long gone and the drivers, now insulated from the interior but responsible for the collection of fares, have no dealings with their customers beyond the purely commercial. There are no cross-London routes: those buses that enter the city terminate halfway across it before returning whence they came, as though to remind their users that this is just another bus service from point A to point B and has no aspiration to map or box or contain or in any other way identify and celebrate London's remarkable scale and diversity, much less its rapidly disappearing belt of protective greenery. Like so much else in Britain today, the Green Line buses merely denote, like a crumbling boundary stone, overgrown and neglected, a past whose purposes and shared experiences are all but lost in Heritage Britain.

VIII

Mimetic Desire

According to the literary theorist René Girard, we come to yearn for and eventually love those who are loved by others. I cannot confirm this from personal experience—I have a history of frustrated longings for objects and women who were palpably unavailable to me but of no particular interest to anyone else. But there is one sphere of my life in which, implausibly, Girard's theory of mimetic desire could be perfectly adapted to my experience: if by "mimetic" we mean mutuality and symmetry, rather than mimicry and contestation, I can vouch for the credibility of his proposition. I love trains, and they have always loved me back.

What does it mean to be loved by a train? Love, it seems to me, is that condition in which one is most contentedly oneself. If this sounds paradoxical, remember Rilke's admonition: love consists in leaving the loved one space to be themselves while providing the security within which that self may flourish. As a child, I always felt uneasy and a little constrained around people, my family in particular. Solitude was bliss, but not easily obtained. *Being* always felt stressful—wherever I was there was something to do, someone to please, a duty to be completed, a role inadequately fulfilled: something amiss. *Becoming*, on the other hand, was relief. I was never so happy as when I was going somewhere on my own, and the longer it took to get there, the better. Walking was pleasurable, cycling enjoyable, bus journeys fun. But the train was very heaven.

I never bothered to explain this to parents or friends, and was thus constrained to feign objectives: places I wanted to visit, people I wanted to see, things I needed to do. Lies, all of it. In those days a child could safely travel on public transport alone from seven years old or so, and I took solitary tube trips around London from a very young age. If I had a goal it was to cover the whole network, from terminus to terminus, an aspiration I came very close to achieving. What did I do when I reached the end of a line, Edgware as it might be, or Ongar? I stepped out, studied the station rather closely, glanced around me, bought a dessicated London Transport sandwich and a Tizer . . . and took the next tube back.

The technology, architecture, and working practices of a railway system fascinated me from the outset—I can describe even today the peculiarities of the separate London Underground lines and their station layouts, the heritage of different private companies in their early years. But I was never a "trainspotter." Even when I graduated to solitary travel on the extensive network of British Railways' Southern Region I never joined the enthusiastic bands of anorak-clad preteenage boys at the end of platforms, assiduously noting down the numbers of the passing trains. This seemed to me the most asinine of static pursuits—the point of a train was to get on it.

The Southern Region in those days offered rich pickings for the lone traveler. I would park my bike in the luggage wagon at Norbiton Station on the Waterloo line, ride the suburban electric train out into rural Hampshire, descend at some little country halt on the slopes of the Downs, cycle leisurely eastward until I reached the westerly edge of the old London to Brighton Railway, then hop the local into Victoria as far as Clapham Junction. There I had the luxuriant choice of some nineteen platforms—this was, after all, the largest rail junction in the world—and would entertain myself with the choices from which to select my train back home. The whole exercise would last a long summer day; when I got home, tired and contented, my parents would inquire politely as to where I had been and I would dutifully invent some worthy purpose to obviate further discussion. My train trips were private and I wanted to keep them that way.

In the Fifties, train travel was cheap—especially for

twelve-year-old boys. I paid for my pleasures from weekly pocket money and still had pennies left over for snacks. The most expensive trip I ever took got me nearly to Dover—Folkestone Central, actually—from where I could look longingly across at the well-remembered *rapides* of the French national network. More typically, I would save spare cash for the Movietone News Theatre at Waterloo Station: London's largest terminus and a cornucopia of engines, timetables, newsstands, announcements, and smells. In later years, I would occasionally miss the last regular train home and sit for hours into the night in Waterloo's drafty waiting halls, listening to the shunting of diesels and the loading of mail, sustained by a single cup of British Rail cocoa and the romance of solitude. God knows what my parents thought I was doing, adrift in London at 2 AM. If they had known, they might have been even more worried.

I was a little too young to capture the thrills of the steam age. The British rail network switched all too soon into diesels (but not electric, a strategic mistake for which it is still paying) and although the great long-distance expresses still swept through Clapham Junction in my early school years, pulled by magnificent late-generation steam engines, most of the trains I took were thoroughly "modern." Nevertheless, thanks to the chronic underinvestment of Britain's nationalized railways, much of the rolling stock dated from interwar years and some of it was pre-1914 vintage. There were separate closed compartments (including one in each four-car unit set aside for "Ladies"), no toilets, and windows held up by leather straps with holes into which a hook in the door was inserted. The seats, even in second- and third-class, were upholstered in a vaguely tartan fabric that irritated the naked thighs of shorts-clad schoolboys but that was comfortingly warm in the damp, chilly winters of those years.

That I should have experienced trains as solitude is of course a paradox. They are, in the French phrase, *transports en commun*: designed from the early-nineteenth-century outset to provide collective travel for persons unable to afford private transportation or, over the years, for the better heeled who could be attracted to luxurious shared accommodations at a higher price. The railways effectively invented social classes in their modern form, by naming and classifying different levels of comfort, facility, and service: as any early illustration can reveal, trains were for many decades crowded and uncomfortable except for those fortunate enough to travel first-class. But by my time second-class was more than acceptable to the respectable middling sort; and in England such persons keep themselves to themselves. In those blissful days before mobile phones, when it was still unacceptable to play a transistor radio in a public place (and the authority of the train conductor sufficed to repress rebellious spirits), the train was a fine and silent place.

In later years, as Britain's rail system fell into decline, train travel at home lost some of its appeal. The privatization of the companies, the commercial exploitation of the stations, and the diminished commitment of the staff all contributed to my disenchantment—and the experience of travel by train in the US was hardly calculated to restore one's memories or enthusiasms. Meanwhile the publicly owned state railways of continental Europe entered a halcyon era of investment and technical innovation, while largely preserving the distinctive qualities inherited from earlier networks and systems.

Thus to travel in Switzerland is to understand the ways in which efficiency and tradition can seamlessly blend to social advantage. Paris's Gare de l'Est or Milano Centrale, no less than Zurich's Hauptbahnhof and Budapest's Keleti Pályaudvar, stand as monuments to nineteenth-century town planning and functional architecture: compare the long-term prospects of New York's inglorious Pennsylvania Station—or virtually any modern airport. At their best—from St. Pancras to Berlin's remarkable new central station—railway stations *are* the very incarnation of modern life, which is why they last so long and still perform so very well the tasks for which they were first designed. As I think back on it—*toutes proportions gardées* Waterloo did for me what country churches and Baroque cathedrals did for so many poets and artists: it inspired me. And why not? Were not the great glass-and-metal Victorian stations the cathedrals of the age?

I had long planned to write about trains. I suppose in a way I have already done so, at least in part. If there is something distinctive about my version of contemporary European history in *Postwar*, it is—I believe—the subliminal emphasis on space: a sense of regions, distances, differences, and contrasts within the limited frame of one small subcontinent. I think I came to that sense of space by staring aimlessly out of train windows and inspecting rather more closely the contrasting sights and sounds of the stations where I alighted. My Europe is measured in train time. The easiest way for me to "think" Austria or Belgium is by meandering around the Westbahnhof or the Gare du Midi and reflecting on the experience, not to mention the distances between. This is certainly not the only way to come to grips with a society and a culture, but it works for me.

Perhaps the most dispiriting consequence of my present disease—more depressing even than its practical, daily manifestations—is the awareness that I shall never again ride the rails. This knowledge weighs on me like a leaden blanket, pressing me ever deeper into that gloom-laden sense of an ending that marks the truly terminal disease: the understanding that some things will never be. This absence is more than just the loss of a pleasure, the deprivation of freedom, much less the exclusion of new experiences. Remembering Rilke, it constitutes the very loss of myself—or at least, that better part of myself that most readily found contentment and peace. No more Waterloo, no more rural country halts, no more solitude: no more becoming, just interminable being.

I X

The Lord Warden

We are all Europeans now. The English travel throughout continental Europe, and the UK is a leading tourist destination as well as a magnet for job seekers from Poland to Portugal. Today's travelers don't think twice before boarding a plane or a train, alighting shortly after in Brussels, Budapest, or Barcelona. True, one European in three never leaves home; but everyone else makes up for them with insouciant ease. Even the (internal) frontiers have melted away: it can be a while before you realize you have entered another country.

It wasn't always thus. In my London childhood, "Europe" was somewhere you went on exotic foreign vacations. The "Continent" was an alien place—I learned far more about New Zealand or India, whose imperial geography was taught in every elementary school. Most people never ventured abroad: vacations were taken at windswept English coastal resorts or in cheery domestic holiday camps. But it was a peculiarity of our family (a side effect of my father's Belgian childhood?) that we crossed the English Channel quite a lot; certainly more than most people in our income bracket.

Celebrities flew to Paris; mere mortals took the boat. There were ferries from Southampton, Portsmouth, Newhaven, Folkestone, Harwich, and points north, but the classic—and by far the most heavily traveled—route lay athwart the neck of the Channel from Dover to Calais or Boulogne. British and French Railways (SNCF) monopolized this crossing until the Sixties. The SNCF still used a pre-war steamer, the SS *Dinard*, which had to be deck-loaded by crane, car by car. This took an extraordinarily long time, even though very few cars used the service in those days. In consequence, my family always tried to schedule trips to coincide with departures by British Railways' flagship ferry, the *Lord Warden*.

Unlike the *Dinard*, a tiny ship that bucked and tossed alarmingly in unsettled seas, the *Lord Warden* was a substantial vessel: capable of handling a thousand passengers and 120 cars. It was named after the Lord Warden of the Cinque Ports—the five coastal settlements granted special freedoms in 1155 AD in return for services to the English Crown. A cross-Channel ferry service from Dover to Calais (an English possession from 1347 until 1558) dated from those same years, so the ship was well-christened.

As I remember it, the *Lord Warden*, which entered service in 1951 and was not retired until 1979, was a spacious modern ship. From its vast vehicle hold to its bright, capacious dining room and leatherette lounges, the boat promised adventure and luxury. I would rush my parents into breakfast, seizing a window table and ogling the ever-so-traditional menu. At home we ate sugarless cereals, drank sugar-free juice, and buttered our wheaten toast with sensible marmalades. But this was holiday-land, a time out of health, and concessions were made.

Half a century later, I still associate continental travel with English breakfast: eggs, bacon, sausages, tomatoes, beans, white-bread toast, sticky jams, and British Railways' cocoa, heaped on heavy white plates emblazoned with the name of the ship and her owners and served by jocular cockney waiters retired from the wartime Merchant Navy. After breakfast, we would clamber up to the broad chilly decks (in those days the Channel seemed unforgivingly cold) and gaze impatiently at the horizon: Was that Cap Gris Nez? Boulogne appeared bright and sunny, in contrast to the low gray mist enshrouding Dover; one disembarked with the misleading impression of having traveled a great distance, arriving not in chilly Picardy but in the exotic South.

Boulogne and Dover were different in ways that are hard to convey today. The languages stood further apart: most people in both towns, despite a millennium of communication and exchange, were monolingual. The shops looked very different: France was still considerably poorer than England, at least in the aggregate. But we had rationing and they did not, so even the lowliest *épiceries* carried foods and drinks unknown and unavailable to envious English visitors. I remember from my earliest days noticing how France *smelled*: whereas the pervading odor of Dover was a blend of frying oil and diesel, Boulogne seemed to be marinated in fish.

It was not necessary to cross the Channel with a car, though the appointment of a purpose-built car ferry was a harbinger of changes to come. You could take the boat train from Charing Cross to Dover Harbour, walk onto the ferry, and descend the gangplank in France directly into a battered old station where the dull green livery and stuffy *compartiments* of French railways awaited you. For the better-heeled or more romantic traveler there was the Golden Arrow: a daily express (inaugurated in 1929) from Victoria to the Gare du Nord, conveyed by track-carrying ferries, its passengers free to remain comfortably in their seats for the duration of the crossing.

Once clear of coastal waters, the purser would announce over the Tannoy that the "shop" was open for purchases.

"Shop," I should emphasize, described a poky cubbyhole at one end of the main deck, identified by a little illuminated sign and staffed by a single cashier. You queued up, put in your request, and awaited your bag—rather like an embarrassed tippler in a Swedish *Systembolaget*. Unless of course you had ordered beyond your duty-free limit, whereupon you would be informed accordingly and advised to reconsider.

The shop did scant business on the outer route: there was little that the *Lord Warden* had to offer that could not be obtained cheaper and better in France or Belgium. But on its passage back to Dover, the little window did a roaring trade. Returning English travelers were entitled to a severely restricted quota of alcohol and cigarettes, so they bought all that they could: the excise duties were punitive. Since the shop remained open for forty-five minutes at most, it cannot have made huge profits—and was clearly offered as a service rather than undertaken as a core business.

In the late 1960s and 1970s, the boats were threatened by the appearance of the Hovercraft, a hybrid floating on an air bubble and driven by twin propellers. Hovercraft companies could never quite decide upon their identity—a characteristic 1960s failing. In keeping with the age, they advertised themselves as efficient and modern—"It's a lot less Bovver with a Hover"—but their "departure lounges" were tacky airport imitations without the promise of flight. The vessels themselves, by obliging you to remain in your seat as they bumped claustrophobically across the waves, suffered all the defects of sea travel while forgoing its distinctive virtues. No one liked them.

Today, the cross-Channel sea passage is serviced by new ships many times the size of the *Lord Warden*. The disposition of space is very different: the formal dining room is relatively small and underused, dwarfed by McDonald's-like cafeterias. There are video game arcades, first-class lounges (you pay at the door), play areas, much-improved toilets . . . and a duty-free hall that would put Safeway to shame. This makes good sense: given the existence of car and train tunnels, not to mention ultra-competitive no-frills airlines, the main motive for taking the boat is to shop.

And so, just as we used to rush for the window seat in the breakfast room, today's ferry passengers spend their journey (and substantial sums of money) buying perfume, chocolate, wine, liquors, and tobacco. Thanks to changes in the tax regime on both sides of the Channel, however, there is no longer any significant economic benefit to duty-free shopping: it is undertaken as an end in itself.

Nostalgics are well-advised to avoid these ferries. On a recent trip I tried to watch the arrival into Calais from the deck. I was tartly informed that all the main decks are kept closed nowadays, and that if I insisted upon staying in the open air I would have to join my fellow eccentrics corralled into a roped-off area on a lower rear platform. From there one could see nothing. The message was clear: tourists were not to waste time (and save money) by wandering the decks. This policy—although it is not applied on the laudably anachronistic vessels of (French-owned) Brittany Ferries—is universally enforced on the short routes: it represents their only hope of solvency.

The days are gone when English travelers watched tearily from the deck as the cliffs of Dover approached, congratulating one another on winning the war and commenting on how good it was to be back with "real English food." But even though Boulogne now looks a lot like Dover (though Dover, sadly, still resembles itself), the Channel crossing continues to tell us a lot about both sides.

Tempted by "loss leader" day-return fares, the English rush to France to buy truckloads of cheap wine, suitcases of French cheese, and carton upon carton of undertaxed cigarettes. Most of them travel by train, transporting themselves or their car through the Tunnel. Upon arrival, they face not the once-forbidding line of customs officers but a welcoming party of giant *hypermarchés*, commanding the hilltops from Dunkerque to Dieppe.

The goods in these stores are selected with a view to British taste—their signs are in English—and they profit mightily from the cross-Channel business. No one is now made to feel remotely guilty for claiming his maximum whisky allowance from a stone-faced sales lady. Relatively few of these British tourists stay long or venture further south. Had they wished to do so, they would probably have taken Ryanair at half the price.

Are the English still unique in traveling abroad for the express purpose of conspicuous down-market consumption? You won't see Dutch housewives clearing the shelves of the Harwich Tesco. Newhaven is no shopper's paradise, and the ladies of Dieppe do not patronize it. Continental visitors debarking at Dover still waste no time in heading for London, their primary objective. But Europeans visiting Britain once sought heritage sites, historical monuments, and culture. Today, they also flock to the winter sales in England's ubiquitous malls.

These commercial pilgrimages are all that most of its citizens will ever know of European union. But proximity can be delusory: sometimes it is better to share with your neighbors a mutually articulated sense of the foreign. For this we require a journey: a passage in time and space in which to register symbols and intimations of change and difference—border police, foreign languages, alien food. Even an indigestible English breakfast may invoke memories of France, implausibly aspiring to the status of a mnemonic madeleine. I miss the *Lord Warden*.

PART TWO

X

Joe

I hated school. From 1959 to 1965 I attended Emanuel
School in Battersea: a Victorian establishment parked
between the railway lines exiting south from Clapham Junction station. The trains (still steam in those days) provided
sound effects and visual relief, but everything else was unremittingly dull. The interior of the older buildings was painted
institutional cream and green—much like the nineteenth-
century hospitals and prisons on which the school was mod-
eled. Scattered postwar embellishments suffered from cheap
materials and inadequate insulation. The playing fields,
though broad and green, seemed to me cold and unfriendly:
no doubt because of the cheerless muscular Christianity that
I came to associate with them.

This grim institution, to which I repaired six times a

week (Saturday morning rugby was compulsory) for nearly seven years, cost my parents nothing. Emanuel was "direct grant": an independent, self-governing secondary school subsidized by the local authorities and open to any boy who did well at the national examinations for eleven-year-olds ("11+") and who was accepted after interview. These establishments, often of venerable vintage (Emanuel had been founded in the reign of Elizabeth I), ranked with the great public schools of England, as well as the best of the state grammar schools whose curriculum they closely followed.

But because most direct grant schools charged no tuition, and because they were usually day schools and thus drew largely upon local talent, their constituency was far down the social ladder from that of Winchester, Westminster, or Eton. Most boys at Emanuel came from the south London lower middle class, with a small number of working-class boys who had done well at the 11+ and a smattering of sons of stockbrokers, bankers, etc. from the outer suburbs who had chosen an inner-city day school over a conventional public school for boarders.

When I arrived in 1959, many of the teachers at Emanuel had been there since the end of World War I: the headmaster, the second master (whose prime responsibility was to oversee the weekly beating of insubordinate small boys by sixth-form prefects), the master of the lower school, and my first English master. The latter, who had arrived in 1920 but whose pedagogical techniques were unmistakably Dickensian, spent most of his time furiously twisting and tweaking the ears of his twelve-year-old pupils. I cannot recall a single thing that he said or that we read in the course of that year; just pain.

The younger teachers were better. Over the years I was reasonably well taught in English literature and mathematics, satisfactorily instructed in history, French, and Latin, and monotonously drilled in nineteenth-century science (if someone had only exposed us to modern biological and physical theories I might have been hungry for the experience). Physical education was neglected, at least by American standards: we took one PE class per week, much of it spent awaiting our turn on the vaulting horse or the wrestling mat. I boxed a little (to please my father, who had boxed a lot and rather successfully); was a passable sprinter; and—to everyone's surprise—turned out to be a better-than-average rugby player. But none of these activities ever caught my imagination or lifted my spirit.

Least of all was I attracted to the absurd "Combined Cadet Force" (CCF), in which small boys were instructed in basic military drill and the use of the Lee Enfield rifle (already obsolete when it was issued to British servicemen in 1916). For nearly five years I went to school each Tuesday in a cut-down World War I British army uniform, enduring the amused stares of fellow commuters and the suppressed giggles of girls on the street. All day we would sit sweltering in our battle dress, only to parade pointlessly around the cricket pitch at the end of classes, harried and bullied by our "sergeants" (older boys) and barked at by "officers" (teachers in uniform enthusiastically reliving their military service at our expense). The whole experience would have put me in mind of Hašek's *Good Soldier Švejk*, had anyone had the wit to point me in that direction.

I was sent to Emanuel because my elementary school headmistress had neglected to prepare me for the entrance examination to St. Paul's, the truly first-rate "public" day school to which my most promising contemporaries were admitted. I don't believe I ever told my mother or father just how unhappy I was at school, except once or twice to relate the endemic anti-Semitism: in those days there were very few "ethnic" minorities in London and Jews were the most visible outsiders. We numbered only ten or so in a school of well over one thousand pupils, and frequent low-level anti-Jewish slurs and name-calling were not particularly frowned upon.

I escaped thanks to King's. In my Cambridge entrance examinations I took not just history but also French and German and was deemed by my future teachers to have performed beyond the level of the high school leaving exams. Upon learning this I wrote immediately to King's to ask whether I might be excused from sitting my A Levels; "yes," they replied. That very day I walked into the school office to announce that I was dropping out. I recall few happier moments and no regrets.

Except perhaps one. At the start of my fourth year at Emanuel, having opted for the "Arts" stream, I was required to choose between German and ancient Greek. Along with everyone else I had been studying French and Latin since my first year; but at the age of fourteen I was deemed ready for "serious" language study. Without giving the matter too much thought I opted for German.

At Emanuel in those days the German language was taught by Paul Craddock: "Joe" to three generations of schoolboys. A gaunt, misanthropic survivor of some unspecified wartime experience—or at least, this was how we accounted for his unpredictable temper and apparent lack of humor. As it happened, Joe had a truly sardonic sense of the absurd, and he was—as I would later learn—a deeply humane person. But his external appearance—all six feet of him, from oversized brogues to unkempt, thinning hair—was terrifying to teenage boys: an invaluable pedagogical asset.

In just two years of intensive German study, I achieved a high level of linguistic competence and confidence. There was nothing mysterious about Joe's teaching methods. We learned by spending hours every day on grammar, vocabulary, and style, in the classroom and at home. There were daily tests of memory, reasoning, and comprehension. Mistakes were ruthlessly punished: to get less than eighteen out of twenty on a vocabulary test was to be "Gormless!" Imperfect grasp of a complicated literary text marked you "Dim as a Toc-H lamp!" (a World War II reference that still meant something—just—to a cohort of teenagers born around 1948). To submit anything short of perfect homework was to doom yourself to a roaring tirade from a wildly gyrating head of angry gray hair, before meekly accepting hours of detention and additional grammatical exercises.

We were terrified of Joe—and yet we adored him. Every time he entered the room, his clanking, bony limbs preceding those baleful, piercing eyes atop a shivering torso, we would fall expectantly silent. There was no praise, no warm fuzzy familiarity or softening of the critical blow. He strode to his desk, slammed down books, flung himself at the blackboard (or else flung the chalk at some insufficiently attentive child), and gave us his all: fifty minutes of intensive, unremitting, undiluted language teaching. In Latin, we were still suffering through *The Gallic Wars*; in French, it had taken us five years to prepare for the national Ordinary Level examinations and learn to translate haltingly from Saint-Exupéry or some comparably accessible text. By halfway through my second year of German, Joe had us translating with consummate ease and real pleasure from Kafka's *Die Verwandlung*.

Despite being one of the (relatively) weaker students in his class—thanks to a distracting interest in Zionism—I did better in O-Level German than in all but one of my other subjects (and much better than I was to do in French or history), securing the second-to-top grade. Joe was character-istically disappointed: he could see no reason why any boy taught German by him should not come top in the country. I dropped German in June 1964. Forty-five years later, I still speak the language passably well, albeit with short-lived memory lapses if I neglect it for too long. I wish I could say the same of other languages I have subsequently learned.

Joe would be impossible today. It is fortunate for him that he was not obliged to earn his living teaching in a modern high school—he was infamously politically in-correct, even by the standards of the age. Understanding full well that the only credible challenge to his monopoly of our attention would be the attractions of the opposite sex, he was brutally dismissive of nascent libidos: "If ye want te play with girls, don't waste my time! You can 'av 'em any time; but this is yer only chance to learn this language and you can't do both. If I even see ye with a girl, yer out of 'ere!" There was only one boy in our class who actually *had* a girlfriend; he was so terrified that Joe might learn of her ex-istence that the poor thing was forbidden to approach within two miles of the school.

Nowadays, almost no one is even taught German. The consensus appears to be that the young mind can handle but one language at a time, preferably the easiest. In American high schools, no less than in Britain's egregiously underper-

forming comprehensive schools, students are urged to believe that they have done well—or at least the best they
could. Teachers are discouraged from distinguishing among
their charges: it is simply not done to do as Joe did and praise
first-rate work while damning the lesser performers. Rarely
are pupils advised that they are "absolute rubbish!" or "the
scum of the earth!"

Fear is at a discount—as is the satisfaction to be had
from sheer, unrelenting linguistic effort. Joe never actually
laid a hand on a boy throughout his long teaching career;
indeed, his classroom was next to the public baths employed
by the homoerotically disposed second master as a beating
ground and he never made any secret of his contempt for the
practice. But his successful deployment of physical intimidation and moral humiliation ("Yer utterly useless!") would be
unavailable to any teacher today, even if he or she were alert
enough to know how to exploit it.

It seems to me significant that in all my unpleasant
memories of school, the one unambiguous positive is the two
years I spent having the German language driven mercilessly
into me. I don't think I am a masochist. If I recall "Joe"
Craddock with such affection and appreciation, it is not
just because he put the fear of God in me or had me parsing
German sentences at 1 AM lest I be dismissed the next day as
"absolute rubbish!" It's because he was the best teacher I ever
had; and being well taught is the only thing worth remembering from school.

XI

Kibbutz

My Sixties were a little different from those of my contemporaries. Of course, I joined in the enthusiasm for the Beatles, mild drugs, political dissent, and sex (the latter imagined rather than practiced, but in this too I think I reflected majority experience, retrospective mythology notwithstanding). But so far as political activism was concerned, I was diverted from the mainstream in the years between 1963 and 1969 by an all-embracing engagement with left-wing Zionism. I spent the summers of 1963, 1965, and 1967 working on Israeli kibbutzim and much of the time in between was actively engaged in proselytizing Labour Zionism as an unpaid official of one of its youth movements. During the summer of 1964 I was being "prepared" for leadership at a training camp in southwest France; and from February through July of 1966 I worked full time at Machanayim, a collective farm in the Upper Galilee.

This decidedly intense sentimental education worked very well at first. At least through the summer of 1967, when I graduated from voluntary work on a kibbutz to auxiliary participation in the Israeli armed forces, I was the ideal recruit: articulate, committed, and uncompromisingly ideologically conformist. Like the circle dancers in Milan Kundera's *Book of Laughter and Forgetting*, I joined with fellow feelers in happy collective revels, excluding dissenters and celebrating our reassuring unity of spirit, purpose, and clothing. I idealized Jewish distinction, and intuitively grasped and reproduced the Zionist emphasis upon separation and ethnic difference. I was even invited—at the absurdly immature age of sixteen—to make a keynote speech to a Zionist youth conference in Paris denouncing smoking as a "bourgeois deviation" and threat to the healthy outdoor commitment of Jewish adolescents. I doubt very much whether I believed this even at the time (I smoked, after all): but I was very good with the words.

The essence of Labour Zionism, still faithful in those years to its founding dogmas, lay in the promise of Jewish work: the idea that young Jews from the diaspora would be rescued from their effete, assimilated lives and transported to remote collective settlements in rural Palestine—there to create (and, as the ideology had it, recreate) a living Jewish peasantry, neither exploited nor exploiting. Derived in equal measure from early-nineteenth-century socialist utopias and later Russian myths of egalitarian village communities, Labour Zionism was characteristically fragmented into conflicting sectarian cults: there were those who believed that everyone on the kibbutz should dress alike, raise their children and eat in common, and use (but not own) identical furniture, household goods, and even books, while deciding collectively upon every aspect of their lives at a mandatory weekly gathering. Softer adaptations of the core doctrine allowed for some variety in lifestyle and even a modicum of personal possessions. And then there were multifarious nuances between kibbutz members, often as not the product of personal or familial conflict recast as fundamentalist discord.

But all were agreed on the broader moral purpose: bringing Jews back to the land and separating them from their rootless diasporic degeneracy. For the neophyte fifteen-year-old Londoner encountering the kibbutz for the first time, the effect was exhilarating. Here was "Muscular Judaism" in its most seductive guise: health, exercise, productivity, collective purpose, self-sufficiency, and proud separatism—not to mention the charms of kibbutz children of one's own generation, apparently free of all the complexes and inhibitions of their European peers (free, too, of most of their cultural baggage—though this did not trouble me until later).

I adored it. Eight hours of strenuous, intellectually
undemanding labor in steamy banana plantations by
the shores of the Sea of Galilee, interspersed with songs,
hikes, lengthy doctrinal discussions (carefully stage-managed
so as to reduce the risk of adolescent rejection while maximizing the appeal of shared objectives), and the ever-present
suggestion of guilt-free sex: in those days the kibbutz and its
accompanying ideological penumbra still retained a hint of
the innocent "free love" ethos of early-twentieth-century
radical cults.

In reality, of course, these were provincial and rather
conservative communities, their ideological rigidity camouflaging the limited horizon of many of their members. Even
in the mid-1960s it was clear that the economy of Israel no
longer rested on small-scale domestic agriculture; and the
care that left-wing kibbutz movements took to avoid employing Arab labor served less to burnish their egalitarian credentials than to isolate them from the inconvenient facts of
Middle Eastern life. I'm sure I did not appreciate all this at
the time—though I do recall even then wondering why I
never met a single Arab in the course of my lengthy kibbutz
stays, despite living in close proximity to the most densely
populated Arab communities of the country.

What I did, however, come quite quickly to understand
if not openly acknowledge was just how limited the kibbutz

and its members really were. The mere fact of collective self-government, or egalitarian distribution of consumer durables, does not make you either more sophisticated or more tolerant of others. Indeed, to the extent that it contributes to an extraordinary smugness of self-regard, it actually reinforces the worst kind of ethnic solipsism.

Even now I can recall my surprise at how little my fellow kibbutzniks knew or cared about the wider world—except insofar as it directly affected them or their country. They were chiefly concerned with the business of the farm, their neighbor's spouse, and their neighbor's possessions (in both cases comparing these enviously with their own). Sexual liberation, on the two kibbutzim where I spent extensive time, was largely a function of marital infidelity and the attendant gossip and recrimination—in which respect these model socialist communities rather closely resembled medieval villages, with similar consequences for those exposed to collective disapproval.

As a result of these observations, I came quite early on to experience a form of cognitive dissonance in the face of my Zionist illusions. On the one hand I wanted deeply to believe in the kibbutz as a way of life and as an incarnation of a better sort of Judaism; and being of a dogmatic persuasion, I had little difficulty convincing myself of its principled virtues for some years. On the other hand, I actively disliked it. I could never wait to get away at the end of a work week, hitchhiking or hopping a bus to Haifa (the nearest significant

city) where I would wile away the Sabbath gorging myself
on sour cream and staring wistfully from the dock at the passenger ferries bound for Famagusta, Izmir, Brindisi, and
other cosmopolitan destinations. Israel felt like a prison in
those days, and the kibbutz like an overcrowded cell.

I was released from my confusions by two quite different developments. When my kibbutz colleagues
learned that I had been accepted into Cambridge University
and planned to attend, they were appalled. The whole culture of "Aliya"—"going up" (to Israel)—presumed the sev-
ering of links and opportunities back in the diaspora. The
leaders of the youth movement in those days knew perfectly
well that once a teenager in England or France was permitted to stay there through university, he or she was probably
lost to Israel forever.

The official position, accordingly, was that university-
bound students should forgo their places in Europe; commit
themselves to the kibbutz for some years as orange pickers,
tractor drivers, or banana sorters; and then, circumstances
permitting, present themselves to the community as candidates for higher education—on the understanding that the
kibbutz would collectively determine what if any course of
studies they should pursue, with the emphasis upon their future usefulness to the collective.

With luck, in short, I might have been sent to college in Israel at the age of twenty-five or so, perhaps to study electrical engineering or, if very fortunate and indulged by my comrades, to train as an elementary teacher of history. At the age of fifteen, this prospect had rather appealed to me. Two years later, having worked hard to get into King's, I had no intention of declining the opportunity, much less abandoning myself to a life in the fields. The utter incomprehension and palpable disdain of the kibbutz community in the face of my decision served merely to confirm my growing alienation from the theory and practice of communitarian democracy.

The other stimulus to separation, of course, was my experience with the army on the Golan Heights after the Six-Day War. There, to my surprise, I discovered that most Israelis were not transplanted latter-day agrarian socialists but young, prejudiced urban Jews who differed from their European or American counterparts chiefly in their macho, swaggering self-confidence, and access to armed weapons. Their attitude toward the recently defeated Arabs shocked me (testament to the delusions of my kibbutz years) and the insouciance with which they anticipated their future occupation and domination of Arab lands terrified me even then. When I returned to the kibbutz on which I was then living—Hakuk in the Galilee—I felt a stranger. Within a few weeks I had packed my bags and headed home. Two years later, in 1969, I returned with my then girlfriend to see what remained. Visiting kibbutz Machanayim I encountered "Uri," a fellow orange picker of earlier days. Without bothering to acknowledge me, much less trouble himself with the usual greetings, Uri passed in front of us, pausing only to demand: *"Ma ata oseah kan?"* ("What are you doing here?") What indeed?

I don't regard those years as squandered or misspent. If anything, they furnished me with a store of memories and lessons somewhat richer than those I might have acquired had I simply passed through the decade in conformity with generational proclivities. By the time I went up to Cambridge I had actually experienced—and led—an ideological movement of the kind most of my contemporaries only ever encountered in theory. I knew what it meant to be a "believer"—but I also knew what sort of price one pays for such intensity of identification and unquestioning allegiance. Before even turning twenty I had become, been, and ceased to be a Zionist, a Marxist, and a communitarian settler: no mean achievement for a south London teenager.

Unlike most of my Cambridge contemporaries, I was thus immune to the enthusiasms and seductions of the New Left, much less its radical spin-offs: Maoism, gauchisme, tiers-mondisme, etc. For the same reasons I was decidedly uninspired by student-centered dogmas of anticapitalist transformation, much less the siren calls of femino-Marxism or sexual politics in general. I was—and remain—suspicious of identity politics in all forms, Jewish above all. Labour Zionism made me, perhaps a trifle prematurely, a universalist social democrat—an unintended consequence which would have horrified my Israeli teachers had they followed my career. But of course they didn't. I was lost to the cause and thus effectively "dead."

XII

Bedder

I grew up without servants. This is hardly surprising: in the first place, we were a small, lower-middle-class family who lived in small, lower-middle-class housing. Before the war, such families could typically afford a maid and perhaps a cook as well. The real middle class, of course, did much better: upstairs and downstairs staff were well within the reach of a professional man and his family. But by the 1950s taxation and higher wages had put domestic employees beyond the reach of all but the best heeled. The most that my parents could aspire to was a day nanny for me—when I was young and my mother worked—followed by a series of au pair girls in the more prosperous later years. Beyond that there was the occasional cleaning lady; nothing more.

I was thus utterly unprepared for Cambridge. In keeping with long tradition, both Oxford and Cambridge universities employed staff whose job was exclusively to look after the young men. In Oxford, such persons were known as "scouts"; in Cambridge, they were "bedders." The distinction was a matter of convention—although the words suggest an interesting nuance in the form of oversight they were required to exercise—but the function was identical. Bedders, like scouts, were expected to prepare a fire (in the days of open-hearth heating), clean the young gentlemen's rooms, make their beds and change their linen, undertake minor shopping expeditions on their behalf, and generally provide them with the services to which they had presumably become accustomed in the course of their upbringing.

To be sure, there were other assumptions implicit in the job description. Oxbridge students, so it was held, were incapable of handling such subaltern tasks: because they had never undertaken them, but also because their aspirations and interests elevated them beyond such concerns. Moreover, and perhaps above all, the bedder was responsible for keeping an eye on the moral condition of her charge (scouts in Oxford were occasionally male, though less so by the 1960s, but bedders in my experience were always women).

I arrived in Cambridge in 1966, by which time the institution of the bedder and the responsibilities placed upon her, though not yet anachronistic, sat in some tension with rapidly shifting cultural mores. In King's, at least, a growing number of students lacked any firsthand acquaintance with domestic servants; we were more than a little confused by the first encounter with a woman who was, at least formally, at our "disposal."

Most bedders were ladies of a certain age, usually from local families who had been in college or university employ for as long as anyone could recall. They were thus intimately familiar with the culture of "service" and the subtle interplay of authority and humility entailed in master–servant relations. In the mid-1960s, there were bedders still on the college rolls who had been there since the armistice of 1918. They knew what to expect of teenage boys: being considerably older than our mothers, they had no trouble extracting the appropriate mix of respect and affection.

But there were also newer, younger bedders. Drawn from the same social class as their older colleagues and likewise rooted in the East Anglian rural community, they doubtless looked upon us as the feckless and privileged outsiders that we were. From our perspective, however, they were decidedly exotic: a girl, often only a few years older than us, who arrived early in the morning and made herself useful in our bedroom. "Useful" in this sense of course was restricted to cleaning up after our mess: while Mrs. (or, as it might be, Miss) Mop fussed benignly around our feet, her plump contours within reach of our adolescent imaginings but otherwise untouchable, we did our best to mimic gentlemen of leisure, slumped carelessly in our armchairs over coffee and newspaper.

The bedder was not fooled of course, nor were we—
though both parties had an interest in pretending
otherwise. The class inhibition (not to mention the risk of unemployment) would have sufficed to constrain the woman. As
for the undergraduate, even if he had no firsthand experience
of this sort of relationship, the sociocultural learning curve was
remarkably steep. By the end of our first semester, we treated
our assigned bedder as though to the manor born.

If the issue of sex arose, it pertained rather to the bedder's implicit duty to enforce (by reporting infractions) the
moral rules and codes of the institution. In most Oxbridge
colleges at that time, girls were rigorously forbidden to
spend the night in a boy's room and had to be out of the
college or hostel by 11 PM or sooner: the authorities took
their in loco parentis responsibilities quite literally. In this as
in most other respects, King's was a little different—not in
its formal regulations so much as in the extent to which they
could be breached with impunity.

Thus most of us at one time or another had a girl in de
facto residence (occasionally serial girls, though not everyone was so blessed): sometimes a fellow student from one of
the three women's colleges, sometimes a trainee teacher or
nurse from the city, not infrequently an import from our
hometown. The college deans and tutors turned a blind eye:
middle-class bohemians themselves, in outlook if not life-

style, they smiled benignly upon breaches of the rules they were expected to enforce—conscious of the college's carefully cultivated self-image of radical dissent and its longstanding tradition of transgressive sexuality (albeit hitherto of the homoerotic variety).

Bedders, of course, saw things differently. Like the college porters and administrative staff, they had often been in their post longer than their employers. Coming from farming or working-class stock, they were also far more morally conservative than the intellectual and professional middle class over whom they exercised informal guardianship and to whom they reported. Caught between naughty young men and their lenient superiors, the bedders of previous decades could fall back on moral convention and public opinion.

But in the Sixties the old rules did not apply—or at least were becoming unenforceable. And so a new set of unstated accords began to emerge, rather like the informal terms on which late-era Communist states were constrained to survive: we pretend to conform and you pretend to believe us. I don't suppose that there were many of us, even by 1968, who would have had the effrontery to present our bedder with not just the evidence of a young lady's presence but the young lady herself. On the other hand, we no longer felt it necessary to strive officiously to cover up our tracks: the occasional item of female attire, or other evidence of overnight companionship, carried scant risk of official censure. We acted as though the bedder supposed us to be living monkishly contemplative lives, and the bedder—complicit and mildly amused—did nothing to disabuse us.

Indeed, the only time I caused my bedder any trouble was the night when I—uncharacteristically and for reasons I no longer recall—returned to my room blind drunk, collapsed onto my bed . . . and woke up in a pool of vomit. Next morning, my bedder, an elderly veteran named Rose, took in the situation with a wordless glance and went to work. Within two hours, I was clean, dressed, and in my armchair, coffee to hand and sputtering with embarrassment. Rose, in cool command, returned my bed and its surroundings to their usual pristine condition while chatting nonchalantly away about her daughter-in-law's travails at the supermarket. She never spoke of the incident to me, nor I to her, and our relationship suffered no detriment.

I think I gave Rose an unusually large box of chocolates that Christmas. I would certainly not have known what else to do: she was poor and might have appreciated hard cash, but the college frowned upon money tips and in any case I was no better off than she was. The difference between us, elective cultural affinities aside, lay in our future prospects, not our contemporary condition. We both understood this, though she doubtless better than I.

A decade later, I was now in authority: Rose's employer, so to speak. A fellow of King's and, briefly, associate dean, it was my job on occasion to reprimand undergraduates for excessively inappropriate behavior. In this capacity I once mediated between a bunch of late-Seventies students (boys and girls alike, King's having gone "mixed" in 1972) who had been seen cavorting naked on the college lawns early one morning and a bedder who had taken umbrage at their immodesty. The students were utterly mystified: in those post-authoritarian times it was incomprehensible to them that anyone would find such behavior untoward, much less "inappropriate." It was not, as one of them pointed out to me, as though they had been "doing it in the road"—a Paul McCartney reference that they could reasonably expect a Sixties-era Fellow to recognize.

The bedder, however, was inconsolable. Nudity was not unfamiliar to her. She had witnessed generations of young rugby players, cavorting drunkenly in their underpants before collapsing into an alcoholic stupor. But this was different. For a start there were girls involved and this upset her. In the second place, no one had made any effort to pretend or dissimulate or cover up. And thirdly, they had laughed at her discomfort. In short, they had broken the rules of engagement and she felt humiliated.

The undergraduates in question, as it turned out, were mostly from state schools: upwardly mobile, first- generation students of modest background. This, too, upset the bedder. It was one thing to be patronized by young gentlemen of the old sort—who would characteristically have apologized the following morning and expressed their regret in the form of a gift or even an affectionate, remorseful embrace. But the newer sort of student treated her as an equal—and it was this as much as anything else which hurt her feelings. The bedder was *not* the undergraduates' equal; never would be. But at least she had a traditional claim, even if only during their student years, upon their forbearance and respect. What was the point of being an underpaid servant if this was no longer forthcoming? At that point the relationship was reduced to one of mere employment, in which case she would be better off at the local canning factory.

The nuances of this encounter would have escaped me altogether had I not myself been educated into this late-era application of noblesse oblige. I tried to explain to the students— just ten years my junior—exactly why this middle-aged lady was so offended and upset. But all they could hear was a justification for indentured servitude in an age of rhetorical egalitarianism. They were certainly not against the institution of bedders, of which they were the beneficiaries. They simply thought that the women should be better paid: as though this would inure them to the injuries of class and the wounded vanity of status loss—absolving the boys and girls whose beds they made from the patronizing obligations of politeness and consideration.

The students faithfully reflected contemporary dispositions. Like the economists of our day—and notwithstanding their own fondly asserted radical predilections—they were of the view that all human relations are best reduced to rational calculations of self-interest. Surely the bedder would rather earn twice as much and agree to turn a blind eye to behavior that she found offensive?

But, as I think back, it was the bedder who showed a more subtle grasp of the core truths of human exchange. The students, unbeknownst to themselves, were parroting a reduced and impoverished capitalist vision: the ideal of monadic productive units maximizing private advantage and indifferent to community or convention. Their bedder knew otherwise. Semiliterate and poorly educated she might have been, but her instincts brought her unerringly to an understanding of social intercourse, the unwritten rules that sustain it, and the a priori interpersonal ethics on which it rests. She had certainly never heard of Adam Smith, but the author of *A Theory of Moral Sentiments* would surely have applauded.

XIII

Paris Was Yesterday

What happened to French intellectuals? Once we had Camus, "the contemporary heir to that long line of moralists whose work perhaps constitutes whatever is most distinctive in French letters" (Sartre). We had Sartre himself. We had François Mauriac, Raymond Aron, Maurice Merleau-Ponty, and the "*inénarrable* Mme De Beauvoir" (Aron). Then came Roland Barthes, Michel Foucault, and—more controversially—Pierre Bourdieu. All could claim significant standing in their own right as novelists, philosophers, or simply "men of letters." But they were also, and above all, French intellectuals.

To be sure, there are still men of very considerable standing outside of France: Jürgen Habermas, for example, or Amartya Sen. But when we think of Habermas, the first thing that comes to mind is his work as a sociologist. Amartya Sen is India's leading intellectual export of the past half-century, but the world knows him as an economist. Otherwise—tumbling a few registers—we have Slavoj i ek, whose rhetorical incontinence suggests an unintentional peripheral parody of the metropolitan original. With i ek—or Antonio Negri, perhaps—we are among intellectuals best known for being . . . intellectual, in the sense that Paris Hilton is famous for being . . . famous.

But for the real thing most people still look to France—or, more precisely, to Paris. Alain Finkielkraut, Julia Kristeva, Pascal Bruckner, André Glucksmann, Régis Debray, and Bernard-Henri Lévy—today's most visible instances—have made their name through serial contributions to controversial or fashionable debates. One and all, they share with each other and their distinctly more illustrious predecessors a capacity to expatiate with confidence across a remarkable spectrum of public and cultural affairs.

Why does this sort of thing get so much more respect in Paris? It would be hard to imagine an American or English director making a film like Éric Rohmer's *Ma Nuit chez Maud* (1969), in which Jean-Louis Trintignant agonizes for nearly two hours over whether or not to sleep with Françoise Fabian, in the process invoking everything from Pascal's bet on the existence of God to the dialectics of Leninist revolution. Here, as in so many French films of that era, indecision rather than action drives forward the plot. An Italian director would have added sex. A German director would have added politics. For the French, ideas sufficed.

The seductive appeal of French intellectuality is undeniable. During the middle third of the twentieth century, every aspiring thinker from Buenos Aires to Bucharest lived in a Paris of the mind. Because French thinkers wore black, smoked Gitanes, talked theory, and spoke French, the rest of us followed suit. I well remember meeting fellow English students in the streets of the Left Bank and switching self-consciously into French. *Précieux*, to be sure, but *de rigueur*.

The very word "intellectual," thus flatteringly deployed, would surely have amused the nationalist writer Maurice Barrès, who first invoked it derisively to describe Émile Zola, Léon Blum, and other defenders of the "Jewish traitor" Dreyfus. Ever since, intellectuals have "intervened" on sensitive public matters, invoking the special authority of their scholarly or artistic standing (today, Barrès himself would be an "intellectual"). It is no accident that nearly all of them attended just one small, prestigious institution: the École Normale Supérieure.

To understand the mystery of French intellectuality, one must begin with the École Normale. Founded in 1794 to train secondary school teachers, it became the forcing house of the republican elite. Between 1850 and 1970, virtually every Frenchman of intellectual distinction (women were not admitted until recently) graduated from it: from Pasteur to Sartre, from Émile Durkheim to Georges Pompidou, from

Charles Péguy to Jacques Derrida (who managed to flunk the exam not once but twice before getting in), from Léon Blum to Henri Bergson, Romain Rolland, Marc Bloch, Louis Althusser, Régis Debray, Michel Foucault, Bernard-Henri Lévy, and all eight French winners of the Fields Medal for mathematics.

When I arrived there in 1970, as a *pensionnaire étranger*, the École Normale still reigned supreme. Unusually for France, it is a residential campus, occupying a quiet block in the midst of the 5th arrondissement. Every student gets his own little bedroom off a quadrangle set around a park-like square. In addition to the dormitories, there are lounges, seminar and lecture rooms, a refectory, a social science library, and the Bibliothèque des Lettres: a magnificent open-shelf library unmatched in its convenience and holdings.

American readers, accustomed to well-stocked research libraries in every land grant university from Connecticut to California, will have trouble grasping what this means: most French universities resemble a badly underfunded community college. But the privileges of *normaliens* extend far beyond their library and bedrooms. Getting into ENS was (and is) quite extraordinarily taxing. Any high school graduate aspiring to admission must sacrifice two additional years being force-fed (the image of geese comes to mind) an intense dose of classical French culture or modern science. He then sits the entrance exam and his performance is ranked against all other candidates, with the results made public. The top hundred or so are offered places in the École—along with a guaranteed lifetime income on the understanding that they pursue careers in the state employ.

Thus, in a population of 60 million, this elite humanist academy trains just three hundred young people at any one time. It is as though all the graduates of all the high schools in the US were pumped through a filter, with less than a thousand of them securing a place at a single college distilling the status and distinction of Harvard, Yale, Princeton, Columbia, Stanford, Chicago, and Berkeley. Unsurprisingly, *normaliens* have a high opinion of themselves.

The young men I met at the École seemed to me far less mature than my Cambridge contemporaries. Gaining admission to Cambridge was no easy matter, but it did not preclude the normal life of a busy youth. However, no one got into the École Normale without sacrificing his teenage years to that goal, and it showed. I was unfailingly astonished by the sheer volume of rote learning on which my French contemporaries could call, suggesting an impacted richness that was at times almost indigestible. *Pâté de foie gras* indeed.

But what these budding French intellectuals gained in culture, they often lacked in imagination. My first breakfast at the École was instructive in this regard. Seated opposite a group of unshaven, pajama-clad freshmen, I buried myself in my coffee bowl. Suddenly an earnest young man resembling the young Trotsky leaned across and asked me (in French): "Where did you do *khâgne* ?"—the high-intensity post-lycée preparatory classes. I explained that I had not done *khâgne*: I came from Cambridge. "Ah, so you did *khâgne* in England." "No," I tried again: "We don't do *khâgne*—I came here directly from an English university."

The young man looked at me with withering scorn. It is not possible, he explained, to enter the École Normale without first undergoing preparation in *khâgne*. Since you are here, you must have done *khâgne*. And with that conclusive Cartesian flourish he turned away, directing his conversation at worthier targets. This radical disjunction between the uninteresting evidence of your own eyes and ears and the incontrovertible conclusions to be derived from first principles introduced me to a cardinal axiom of French intellectual life.

B ack in 1970 the École boasted quite a few self-styled "Maoists." One of them, a talented mathematician, took pains to explain to me why the great Bibliothèque des Lettres should be razed to the ground:" *Du passé faisons table rase*" ("let's make a clean slate of the past"). His logic was impeccable: the past is indeed an impediment to unrestricted innovation. I found myself at a loss to explain just why it would be a mistake all the same. In the end I simply told him that he would see things differently in years to come. "A very English conclusion," he admonished me.

My Maoist friend and his colleagues never did burn down the library (though a halfhearted attempt was made one night to storm it). Unlike their German and Italian counterparts, the radical fringe of the French student movement never passed from revolutionary theorizing to violent practice. It would be interesting to speculate why this was: the rhetorical violence certainly attained a considerable pitch in the year I was there, with Maoist *normaliens* periodically "occupying" the dining hall and covering it with slogans: *les murs ont la parole*. Yet they failed to make common cause with similarly "angry" students down the road in the Sorbonne.

This should not surprise us. To be a *normalien* in Paris in those days conferred upon you considerable cultural capital, as Pierre Bourdieu (another *normalien*) would have put it. *Normaliens* had more to lose than most European students by turning the world upside down, and they knew it. The image (imported from Central Europe) of the intellectual as rootless cosmopolitan—a class of superfluous men at odds with an unsympathetic society and repressive state—never applied in France. Nowhere were intellectuals more *chez eux*.

Raymond Aron, who arrived at the École in 1924, wrote in his *Mémoires* that "I have never met so many intelligent men gathered in such a small space." I would second that sentiment. Most of the *normaliens* I knew have gone on to glorious academic or public careers (the outstanding exception being Bernard-Henri Lévy, of whom I suppose it might all the same be said that he too fulfilled his promise). But with certain notable exceptions they remain strikingly homogeneous as a cohort: gifted, brittle, and curiously provincial.

In my day, Paris was the intellectual center of the world. Today it feels marginal to the international conversation. French intellectuals still generate occasional heat, but such light as they emit comes to us from a distant sun— perhaps already extinct. Symptomatically, ambitious young Frenchmen and women today attend the École Nationale d'Administration: a forcing house for budding bureaucrats. Or else they go to business school. Young *normaliens* are as brilliant as ever, but they play little part in public life (neither Finkielkraut nor Glucksmann, Bruckner nor Kristeva attended the École). This seems a pity. Intellectual sheen was not France's only trump card but—like the language itself, another waning asset—it was distinctive. Are the French well served by becoming just like us, only a little less so?

Thinking back on my time at Normale Sup' I am reminded of the engineer (a graduate of the École Polytechnique, Normale's counterpart in the applied sciences) who was sent by his king in 1830 to observe the trials of George Stephenson's "Rocket" on the newly opened Manchester– Liverpool railway line. The Frenchman sat by the track taking copious notes as the sturdy little engine faultlessly pulled the world's first railway train back and forth between the two cities. After conscientiously calculating what he had just observed, he reported his findings back to Paris: "The thing is impossible," he wrote. "It cannot work." Now *there* was a French intellectual.

XIV

Revolutionaries

I was born in England in 1948, late enough to avoid conscription by a few years, but in time for the Beatles: I was fourteen when they came out with "Love Me Do." Three years later the first miniskirts appeared: I was old enough to appreciate their virtues, young enough to take advantage of them. I grew up in an age of prosperity, security, and comfort—and therefore, turning twenty in 1968, I rebelled. Like so many baby boomers, I conformed in my nonconformity.

Without question, the 1960s were a good time to be young. Everything appeared to be changing at unprecedented speed and the world seemed to be dominated by young people (a statistically verifiable observation). On the other hand, at least in England, change could be deceptive. As students we vociferously opposed the Labour government's support for Lyndon Johnson's war in Vietnam. I recall at least one such protest in Cambridge, following a talk there by Denis Healey, the defense minister of the time. We chased his car out of the town—a friend of mine, now married to the EU high commissioner for foreign affairs, leaped onto the hood and hammered furiously at the windows.

It was only as Healey sped away that we realized how late it was—college dinner would start in a few minutes and we did not want to miss it. Heading back into town, I found myself trotting alongside a uniformed policeman assigned to monitor the crowd. We looked at each other. "How do you think the demonstration went?" I asked him. Taking the question in stride—finding in it nothing extraordinary—he replied: "Oh I think it went quite well, Sir."

Cambridge, clearly, was not ripe for revolution. Nor was London: at the notorious Grosvenor Square demonstration outside the American embassy (once again about Vietnam—like so many of my contemporaries I was most readily mobilized against injustice committed many thousands of miles away), squeezed between a bored police horse and some park railings, I felt a warm, wet sensation down my leg. Incontinence? A bloody wound? No such luck. A red paint bomb that I had intended to throw in the direction of the embassy had burst in my pocket.

That same evening I was to dine with my future mother-in-law, a German lady of impeccably conservative instincts.

I doubt if it improved her skeptical view of me when I arrived at her door covered from waist to ankle in a sticky red substance—she was already alarmed to discover that her daughter was dating one of those scruffy lefties chanting "Ho, Ho, Ho Chi Minh" whom she had been watching with some distaste on television that afternoon. I, of course, was only sorry that it was paint and not blood. Oh to *épater la bourgeoisie.*

For real revolution, of course, you went to Paris. Like so many of my friends and contemporaries I traveled there in the spring of 1968 to observe—to inhale—the genuine item. Or, at any rate, a remarkably faithful performance of the genuine item. Or, perhaps, in the skeptical words of Raymond Aron, a psychodrama acted out on the stage where once the genuine item had been performed in repertoire. Because Paris really had been the site of revolution—indeed, much of our visual understanding of the term derives from what we think we know of the events there in the years 1789–1794—it was sometimes difficult to distinguish between politics, parody, pastiche . . . and performance.

From one perspective everything was as it should be: real paving stones, real issues (or real enough to the participants), real violence, and occasionally real victims. But at another level it all seemed not quite serious: even then I was hard pushed to believe that beneath the paving stones lay the beach (*sous les pavés la plage*), much less that a community of students shamelessly obsessed with their summer travel plans—in the midst of intense demonstrations and debates, I recall much talk of Cuban vacations—seriously intended to overthrow President Charles de Gaulle and his Fifth Republic. All the same, it was their own children out on the streets, so many French commentators purported to believe this might happen and were duly nervous.

By any serious measure, nothing at all happened and we all went home. At the time, I thought Aron unfairly dismissive—his dyspepsia prompted by the sycophantic enthusiasms of some of his fellow professors, swept off their feet by the vapid utopian clichés of their attractive young charges and desperate to join them. Today I would be disposed to share his contempt, but back then it seemed a bit excessive. The thing that seemed most to annoy Aron was that everyone was having *fun*—for all his brilliance he could not see that even though having fun is not the same as making a revolution, many revolutions really did begin playfully and with laughter.

A year or two later I visited a friend studying at a German university—Göttingen, I believe. "Revolution" in Germany, it turned out, meant something very different. No one was having fun. To an English eye, everyone appeared unutterably serious—and alarmingly preoccupied with sex. This was something new: English students thought a lot about sex but did surprisingly little; French students were far more sexually active (as it seemed to me) but kept sex and politics quite separate. Except for the occasional exhortation to "make love, not war," their politics were intensely—even absurdly—theoretical and dry. Women participated—if at all—as coffee makers and sleeping partners (and as shoulder-borne visual accessories for the benefit of press photographers). Little wonder that radical feminism followed in short order.

But in Germany, politics was about sex—and sex very largely about politics. I was amazed to discover, while visiting a German student collective (all the German students I knew seemed to live in communes, sharing large old apartments and each other's partners), that my contemporaries in the Bundesrepublik really believed their own rhetoric. A rigorously complex-free approach to casual intercourse was, they explained, the best way to rid oneself of any illusions about American imperialism—and represented a therapeutic purging of their parents' Nazi heritage, characterized as repressed sexuality masquerading as nationalist machismo.

The notion that a twenty-year-old in Western Europe might exorcise his parents' guilt by stripping himself (and his partner) of clothes and inhibitions—metaphorically casting off the symbols of repressive tolerance—struck my empirical English leftism as somewhat suspicious. How fortunate that anti-Nazism required—indeed, was defined by—serial orgasm. But on reflection, who was I to complain? A Cambridge student whose political universe was bounded by

deferential policemen and the clean conscience of a victori-
ous, unoccupied country was perhaps ill-placed to assess
other peoples' purgative strategies.

I might have felt a little less superior had I known
more about what was going on some 250 miles to the
east. What does it say of the hermetically sealed world of cold
war Western Europe that I—a well-educated student of history, of East European Jewish provenance, at ease in a number of foreign languages, and widely traveled in my half of
the continent—was utterly ignorant of the cataclysmic events
unraveling in contemporary Poland and Czechoslovakia? Attracted to revolution? Then why not go to Prague, unquestionably the most exciting place in Europe at that time? Or
Warsaw, where my youthful contemporaries were risking ex-
pulsion, exile, and prison for their ideas and ideals?

What does it tell us of the delusions of May 1968 that I
cannot recall a single allusion to the Prague Spring, much less
the Polish student uprising, in all of our earnest radical debates? Had we been less parochial (at forty years' distance, the
level of intensity with which we could discuss the injustice of
college gate hours is a little difficult to convey), we might
have left a more enduring mark. As it was, we could expatiate
deep into the night on China's Cultural Revolution, the Mex-
ican upheavals, or even the sit-ins at Columbia University.

But except for the occasional contemptuous German who was content to see in Czechoslovakia's Dubček just another reformist turncoat, no one talked of Eastern Europe.

Looking back, I can't help feeling we missed the boat. Marxists? Then why weren't we in Warsaw debating the last shards of Communist revisionism with the great Leszek Kołakowski and his students? Rebels? In what cause? At what price? Even those few brave souls of my acquaintance who were unfortunate enough to spend a night in jail were usually home in time for lunch. What did we know of the courage it took to withstand weeks of interrogation in Warsaw prisons, followed by jail sentences of one, two, or three years for students who had dared to demand the things we took for granted?

For all our grandstanding theories of history, then, we failed to notice one of its seminal turning points. It was in Prague and Warsaw, in those summer months of 1968, that Marxism ran itself into the ground. It was the student rebels of Central Europe who went on to undermine, discredit, and overthrow not just a couple of dilapidated Communist regimes but the very Communist idea itself. Had we cared a little more about the fate of ideas we tossed around so glibly, we might have paid greater attention to the actions and opinions of those who had been brought up in their shadow.

No one should feel guilty for being born in the right place at the right time. We in the West were a lucky generation. We did not change the world; rather, the world changed obligingly for us. Everything seemed possible: unlike young people today we never doubted that there would be an interesting job for us, and thus felt no need to fritter away our time on anything as degrading as "business school." Most of us went on to useful employment in education or public service. We devoted energy to discussing what was wrong with the world and how to change it. We protested the things we didn't like, and we were right to do so. In our own eyes at least, we were a revolutionary generation. Pity we missed the revolution.

XV

Work

I always wanted to be a historian. I was twelve when I began calculating how long it would take to accumulate the necessary degrees. How did historians earn a living? The only one my family had ever seen was A.J.P. Taylor—and while I assumed that he got paid for his stylish television lectures, I never supposed that most historians got by thus. How did one make a "career" in history? Indeed, how does one "make a career"? Do you plan it, starting at puberty? Does it just happen? What if it doesn't? There was a future in there somewhere, but until then I had to earn money.

My first job was in the music department of W.H. Smith Booksellers in London: at fourteen, I was only permitted to work Saturdays. The chief attraction was seventeen-year-old

April. She ran the counter and resembled Janis, the television pop music panelist who acquired fleeting national celebrity for her trademark assessment of the latest pap: "Oi'll give it foive!"

We were still BBE (Before Beatles Era) and the shelves were stocked with forgettable Elvis imitations. The American originals—Gene Vincent, Eddie Cochrane—were a cut above their pale English counterparts (Cliff Richard, already something of a joke, Adam Faith, and a dozen others). Jazz was a minority taste, folk virtually unknown—at least in Putney High Street, where I worked. It was 1962 but the 1950s were still going strong.

Four years later, having secured a place at Cambridge, I dropped out of high school and arranged to work my passage to Israel on a freighter. The boat was due to pass through the Kiel Canal, which bisects the Holstein peninsula a few kilometers north of Hamburg. Tramp steamers keep irregular schedules—when I arrived at the Kiel docks the *Hechalutz* (en route from Gdansk) was nowhere to be seen: it was "expected." I found a bed in a local hostel, checking the port and the canal locks every few hours.

Kiel was grim. Wartime damage had been made good, but the result—as so often in postwar West Germany—was a charmless urban space shorn of history or variety. The hostel was unwelcoming: expelled onto the streets directly after breakfast, I was not readmitted until dusk. My money was stolen by a fellow resident; nocturnal visits to the dock, awaiting the incoming tide and its attendant ships, were fueled by sausage sandwiches—courtesy of a sympathetic stall-keeper. At last, the *Hechalutz* loomed through the Baltic mist. For an indulgent moment, shoulders hunched against the wind, I saw myself as Gabin in a Marcel Carné film: *Le Quai des Brumes*, perhaps.

The captain greeted me suspiciously. I was on his manifest, but he had no idea what to make of this eighteen-year-old wayfarer. "What can you do?" he asked. "Well," I responded, "I speak French, German, and some Hebrew"—as though applying for a temping job in a translation agency. "Me too; *az ma* (so what)?" came the contemptuous reply. I was shown my cabin and told to report to the engine room the following morning. There, and for the next four weeks, I worked the 8 AM–4 PM shift down among the deafening pistons. A diesel engine on an ocean-going vessel is largely self-maintaining: there was just one engineer on duty, overseeing the assorted dials, levers—and me. The machinery emitted a thick film of grease. My job was to clean it.

For the first few days I alternated between scrubbing diesel boilers and throwing up in the teeth of a North Sea blizzard. Eventually I acclimatized. There was no choice—I could not have graduated to deck work. The bosun (a sullen Israeli, built like a dwarf tank) did once order me to roll some barrels under cover in anticipation of an approaching squall. I could not budge them and was dismissively returned to my subterranean labors. On the last night of the voyage, the captain called me in and gruffly acknowledged that he was surprised: "I never thought you would last." Me neither, I silently conceded.

Unskilled manual labor on a ship had its compensations. I spent the graveyard watch up on the bridge with the third mate, a few years my senior, listening to pirated pop music transmitted from Spain, Portugal, and Morocco, as the little boat pitched into the storms and swells of the eastern Atlantic. In Cyprus I was introduced to "the nicest ladies in Famagusta" and that same evening (as the youngest person aboard) shaved my mustache and dressed up as "the nicest lady on the *Hechalutz*" for the entertainment of the suspiciously enthusiastic crew. My very own sentimental education.

B ack home, working in a Sussex brickyard, I revised my views on manual labor: there is nothing noble about unskilled physical work. It is hard and dirty and mostly unrewarding; the incentive to avoid supervision, cut corners, and do the minimum is rational and irresistible. As soon as I could, I swapped the brickyard for a series of driving jobs: semiskilled—though no better paid—these at least afforded me autonomy and privacy. Between 1966 and 1970 I worked variously as a deliverer of carpets, warehouse supplies, and domestic dry goods.

Looking back on my days ferrying groceries around south London, I am struck by how compact the orders were.

A typical household would take no more than two small boxes a week. For everything else the housewife shopped daily at a neighborhood greengrocer, dairy, butcher, or poulterer. Supermarkets were almost unknown. Bulk purchases made no sense: most people had tiny refrigerators, some had none at all. In my green Morris van, the grocer's family name proudly emblazoned on its side, I could carry up to two dozen orders at a go. Today, a typical outing to the mall would fill the little Morris with one household's weekly supplies.

For two summers at the end of the 1960s I abandoned my trucks for guided tours, escorting American student tourists around Western Europe. The pay was moderate, the benefits distinctive. In those days, girls from nice American families did not travel overseas alone; parents preferred to reward graduation with a European holiday in the company of like-minded young women and a reliable chaperone.

The company I worked for boasted of employing only Oxbridge undergraduates: mysteriously, we were thought uniquely suited to the task of escorting upward of forty American coeds on a nine-week vacation. All of the girls on these tours were either in college or had recently completed it, yet none of them had ever traveled outside the continental US. Europe, even the best-known bits (Paris, London, Rome), was utterly unfamiliar.

One night in the Waldstätterhof Seehotel on Lake Lucerne, I was awoken at 5 AM by a panic-stricken tour member. "Come quickly—someone's trying to break in to Lizbeth's room!" Two floors down, the night porter was hammering angrily at a bedroom door, incoherently sputtering a man's name. I brushed him aside, announced myself, and was let in. Lizbeth was standing on the bed wearing nothing very much. "He's going to kill us!" she hissed. Us? She pointed at the cupboard from which emerged a blond-haired young man in underpants: the hotel sous-chef. "It's me he wants," the boy explained sheepishly in German. I conveyed the situation to his American host; she was utterly bewildered. "There are men," I clarified, "who are attracted to other men." Magnificently indifferent to her diaphanous appearance, Lizbeth stared at me in disgust: "Not in Biloxi there aren't."

This was July 1968. In Munich later that month, I instructed our German bus driver to take us to the Dachau memorial. Horst refused point-blank: nothing worth seeing there, he assured me, and anyway it's all American propaganda. The Holocaust and the camps were not yet a universal moral reference, and there were no homosexuals in Mississippi. It was all a long time ago.

My last job was at the Blue Boar, a hotel then gracing the center of Cambridge. Responsible for breakfasts, I worked the kitchen from 5:30 AM until the lunch crew arrived. There were no coeds, but otherwise it was the ideal nonacademic appointment. Like Czech intellectuals consigned to boiler rooms in the years of "normalization" (but in my case by choice), I found this sort of work ideally suited to serious reading. Between preparing the toast, boiling the coffee, and frying the eggs for traveling salesmen and visiting parents, I read much of the background material for my doctoral dissertation. Once mastered, short-order cooking does more than allow for the life of the mind: it facilitates it.

Conversely, the para-academic drudgery normally forced upon impecunious scholars—high school history coaching, adjunct lecturing, or exam grading (I have done them all)—occupies the mind while offering no intrinsic satisfaction. You can think complicated thoughts while trundling a lorry-load of carpets around the suburbs; but working against the clock to grade exams by the page leaves room for little else.

From the Blue Boar, I went directly to a Fellowship at King's College, Cambridge. There was nothing inevitable about this: I had been rejected from Fellowship competitions everywhere I applied and would surely have taken up permanent employment of a very different sort had King's not rescued me. The serendipity of this outcome left me with a lasting insight into the precariousness of careers: everything might have been different.

I don't suppose I would have spent the rest of my life making toast at the Blue Boar, delivering carpets, or cleaning diesel engines. It's even unlikely that I would have made a career out of escorting young women around Europe, however tempting. But it seemed that I might have to fall back on one or more of these for an indefinite period—a prospect that has left me distinctly sympathetic to those who, for reasons of chance or misfortune, find themselves on the wrong side of the line.

We remain in thrall to the industrial-era notion that our work defines us: but this is palpably untrue for the overwhelming majority of people today. If we must invoke nineteenth-century clichés, better to recall "The Right to Laziness": an unintentionally prescient 1883 pamphlet by Marx's son-in-law Paul Lafargue suggesting that modern life will offer ever more opportunities for self-definition through leisure and avocation. Mere employment will occupy a thankfully diminishing role.

I ended up doing what I had always wanted to—and getting paid for it. Most people are not so fortunate. The majority of jobs are tedious: they neither enrich nor sustain. All the same (like our Victorian predecessors), we once again regard unemployment as a shameful condition: something akin to a character defect. Well-paid pundits are quick to lecture "welfare queens" on the moral turpitude of economic dependence, the impropriety of public benefits, and the virtues of hard work. They should try it some time.

XVI

Meritocrats

I came up to King's College, Cambridge, in 1966. Ours was a—perhaps *the*—transitional generation. We were past the midpoint of the 1960s—the Mods had come and gone and the Beatles were about to record *Sgt. Pepper*— but the King's into which I was matriculated was still strikingly traditional. Dinner in Hall was formal, begowned—and required. Undergraduates took their seats, awaited the arrival of the Fellows, then rose to watch a long line of elderly gentlemen shuffle past them on their way to High Table.

"Elderly" here is no relative term. Led by (former provost) Sir John Shepherd (born 1881), the Emeritus Fellows typically included Sir Frank Adcock (born 1886), E. M. Forster (born 1879), and others equally venerable. One was made immediately aware of the link between a generation of young men born into the postwar welfare state and the world of late-Victorian King's: the age of Forster, Rupert Brooke, and John Maynard Keynes, exuding a cultural and social self-confidence to which we could never aspire. The old men seemed to blend seamlessly into the fading portraits on the walls above: without anyone making a point of it, continuity was all about us.

And yet, we were a path-breaking cohort. By the time we graduated, gowns, caps, gate hours, and a whole rulebook of minor regulations—all of them in place when we arrived—were the object of amused nostalgia. In my first term, an enthusiastic if mediocre rugby player, I took the team bus to Oxford to play (and lose to) New College. We got back late, courtesy of a half-successful attempt to dismantle one of our host's urinals, and some late autumn fog. I arrived at the entrance to my hostel: it was locked—and I had no "late pass." A flurry of stones succeeded in waking up a friend, who came down utterly petrified: "Don't let the warden hear you!" It goes without saying that this story would be hard to explain to a King's student today; but it would have been equally implausible to someone who arrived two years after us. The change came suddenly.

King's prided itself on the enthusiasm with which it embraced change and radical disruption. The senior tutor of the day would explain to freshmen that locked gates and disciplinary regulations should be regarded with a wink and a nod. This seemed a little rough on the porters and hostel wardens who were responsible for enforcing them—an early introduction to the subtlety of social rank at Cambridge: middle-class bohemians themselves in outlook if not lifestyle, most college officers smiled benignly upon breaches of the rules they were expected to uphold.

The college was also responsible for the appalling new student bar installed shortly after we arrived. Abreast of contemporary style in all things, the Fellows approved a design that resembled nothing so much as the departure lounge at Gatwick Airport—and was chosen for just that reason: King's (founded in 1441) was not to dwell on its heritage, especially now that it had so many young men for whom the upper-class milieu of Oxbridge meant nothing. As one of those "new" Kingsmen—the first person in my family to complete secondary school, much less attend university — I can say that I would have far preferred the stuffed ambience of a nineteenth-century gentlemen's club to the ersatz classlessness of the bar. Fortunately this experiment was not representative. The college maintained sufficient self-confidence to offer its students a reassuring sense of continuity and identity.

To me, a South Londoner who had never been north of Leicester, our generation of Kingsmen was not just socially mixed but geographically heterogeneous. For the first time I met boys from the Wirral, Yorkshire, Tyneside, East Anglia, and the Celtic fringe. To a remarkable degree, they were—like me—the upwardly mobile products of selective state schools without fees: we had the 1944 Butler Education Act to thank for our presence in Cambridge, although for some of us the social gulf to be bridged was substantial indeed. The mother of John Bentley, the first boy to attend Kings from a comprehensive school,[1] explained to my parents at our graduation party that whenever people on her street asked where her son was and what he was doing, she was tempted to reply that he was "back in Borstal,"[2] a more convincing and ultimately respectable answer than confessing that he was punting girls around on the Cambridge Backs.

Somewhere else in the college there surely lurked enclaves of elite private school boys; perhaps they were in the majority? But I only ever became closely acquainted with one such person—my neighbor Martyn Poliakoff, great-grandnephew of the Poliakoff who built the Russian railways, a spiky-haired eccentric out of Westminster School who went on to secure a CBE, Fellowship of the Royal Society, and deserved renown as a popularizer of chemistry to young people. Hardly your typical toff.

My King's was the very incarnation of meritocratic postwar Britain. Most of us got where we were by doing well in exams and, to a striking extent, we pursued occupations that reflected our early talents and interests. The cohort of Kingsmen who came up in 1966 stand out in their choice of careers: more than any group before or since, we opted for education, public service, the higher reaches of journalism, the arts, and the unprofitable end of the liberal professions.

It is thus altogether appropriate that the most promising economist of our generation—Mervyn King—should have ended up as the governor of the Bank of England, rather than an investment banker or hedge funder. Before our time, talented Kingsmen doubtless followed similar paths. But a glance at the obituaries of an older generation reveals just how many of them returned to the family business or to the traditional professions of their fathers and grandfathers.

As for those who came after, it is depressing to record how quickly and in what numbers the graduates of the 1970s and since resorted to the world of private banking, commerce, and the more remunerative reaches of the law. Perhaps one should not blame them; in our time, jobs were still plentiful and we could bask in the waning rays of postwar prosperity. All the same, it's very clear that our elective affinities lay elsewhere.

I used to ask my contemporaries why they opted for King's. A surprising number had no clear response: they just picked it by name, because they admired the chapel or because it sounded distinctive. A handful—mostly economists—said it was because of Keynes. But I was directed to apply to King's for very specific reasons. A rebel at school—I dropped out in the second year of the 6th form—I was tartly assured by my teachers that no other college in Oxbridge would give me the time of day. But King's, they seemed to feel, was sufficiently oddball to find me a congenial candidate. I have no idea whether any other college would have considered my application; fortunately, I never had to find out.

College teaching was idiosyncratic. Most of my supervisors—John Saltmarsh, Christopher Morris, and Arthur Hibbert—were obscure, published little, and known only to generations of Kingsmen. Thanks to them I acquired not just a patina of intellectual self-confidence, but abiding respect for teachers who are indifferent to fame (and fortune) and to any consideration outside the supervision armchair.

We were never taught with the specific aim of performing well on the Tripos—the Cambridge final examinations. My supervisors were supremely uninterested in public performance of any sort. It was not that they were indifferent to exam results; they simply took it for granted that our natural talent would carry us through. It's hard to imagine such people today, if only because they would be doing the college a profound financial disservice in the face of the Research Assessment Exercise, whereby the British government assesses "academic output" and disburses funds accordingly.

Perhaps I am ill-placed to assess the 1960s in King's. I went on to do graduate work there and held a fellowship for six years, before decamping for Berkeley in 1978: my memories are side-shadowed by later developments. The King's of Noel Annan—provost from 1956 to 1966—was giving way to that of Edmund Leach (1966–1979), an internationally renowned anthropologist of the Levi-Strauss school. The unmediated self-confidence of the Annan generation[3] would be replaced by a certain ironic distance: you never quite felt with Provost Leach that he cared deeply or believed implicitly in the college as a repository of all that was best in Edwardian liberal dissent. For him it was just another myth ripe for the unraveling.

But what Leach did stand for—more than Annan and certainly more than the intellectually undistinguished John Shepherd—was pure smarts: an emphasis further accentuated when Leach was succeeded by the incomparable Bernard Williams. I served for a while as a very junior member on the College Fellowship Electors with Williams, John Dunn, Sydney Brenner (the Nobel Prize winner in medicine), Sir Frank Kermode, Geoffrey Lloyd (the historian of ancient science), and Sir Martin Rees (the Astronomer Royal). I have never lost the sense that *this* was learning: wit, range, and above all the ability (as Forster put it in another context) to connect.

My greatest debt, though I did not fully appreciate it at the time, was to Dunn, then a very young college Research Fellow, now a distinguished professor emeritus. It was John who—in the course of one extended conversation on the political thought of John Locke—broke through my well-armored adolescent Marxism and first introduced me to the challenges of intellectual history. He managed this by the simple device of listening very intently to everything I said, taking it with extraordinary seriousness on its own terms, and then picking it gently and firmly apart in a way that I could both accept and respect.

That is teaching. It is also a certain sort of liberalism: the kind that engages in good faith with dissenting (or simply mistaken) opinions across a broad political spectrum. No doubt such tolerant intellectual breadth was not confined to King's. But listening to friends and contemporaries describe their experiences elsewhere, I sometimes wonder. Lecturers in other establishments often sounded disengaged and busy, or else professionally self-absorbed in the manner of American academic departments at their least impressive.

There is more of that in King's today than there used to be. As in so many other respects, I think our generation was fortunate: we got the best of both worlds. Promoted on merit into a class and culture that were on their way out, we experienced Oxbridge just before the fall—for which I confess that my own generation, since risen to power and office, is largely responsible.

For forty years, British education has been subjected to a catastrophic sequence of "reforms" aimed at curbing its elitist inheritance and institutionalizing "equality."

The havoc wrought in higher education was well summarized by Anthony Grafton in this magazine,[4] but the worst damage has been at the secondary level. Intent upon destroying the selective state schools that afforded my generation a first-rate education at public expense, politicians have foisted upon the state sector a system of enforced downward uniformity.

The result, predicted from the outset, was that the selective private schools ("public schools") have flourished. Desperate parents pay substantial fees to exempt their children from dysfunctional state schools; universities are under inordinate pressure to admit underqualified candidates from the latter and have lowered their admissions standards accordingly; each new government has instituted reforms aimed at compensating for the failed "initiatives" of their predecessors.

Today, when the British government mandates that 50 percent of high school graduates should attend university, the gap separating the quality of education received by the privately schooled minority from that of everyone else is greater than at any time since the 1940s. They consistently outperform their state-educated peers—a dirty little secret that no one cares to acknowledge but that panicked New Labour governments. It does seem curious to curse the private schools for thriving in a market while enthusiastically rewarding bankers for doing so.

Successive education ministers have authorized and encouraged "academies"—furtively reintroducing (with the help of private money) the very process of selection of whose abolition on egalitarian grounds they once so proudly boasted. Meanwhile, we now have more private school graduates in the British cabinet than for decades past (seventeen at my count)—and the first old Etonian prime minister since 1964. Perhaps we should have stuck with meritocracy.

On my occasional return trips to Cambridge, I am struck by the air of doubt and decline. Oxbridge has certainly not resisted the demagogic vogue: what began as ironic self-mockery in the 1970s ("Here at King's we have five hundred years of rules and traditions but we don't take them very seriously, Ha! Ha!") has become genuine confusion. The earnest self-interrogatory concern with egalitarianism that we encountered in 1966 appears to have descended into an unhealthy obsession with maintaining appearances as the sort of place that would never engage in elitist selection criteria or socially distinctive practices of any kind.

I'm not sure that there is anything to be done about this. King's, like much else in contemporary Britain, has become a heritage site. It celebrates an inheritance of dissidence, unconvention, and unconcern for hierarchy: look at us—aren't we *different*. But you cannot celebrate your qualities of uniqueness unless you have a well-grounded appreciation of what it was that gave them distinction and value. Institutions need substantive traditions and I fear that King's—like Oxbridge at large—has lost touch with its own.

I suspect that all this began precisely in those transitional years of the mid-1960s. We, of course, understood nothing of that. We got both the traditions *and* the transgressions; the continuities *and* the change. But what we bequeathed to our successors was something far less substantial than what we ourselves had inherited (a general truth about the baby-boom generation). Liberalism and tolerance, indifference to external opinion, a prideful sense of distinction accompanying progressive political allegiances: these are manageable contradictions, but only in an institution unafraid to assert its particular form of elitism.

Universities *are* elitist: they are about selecting the most able cohort of a generation and educating them to their ability—breaking open the elite and making it consistently anew. Equality of opportunity and equality of outcome are not the same thing. A society divided by wealth and inheritance cannot redress this injustice by camouflaging it in educational institutions—by denying distinctions of ability or by restricting selective opportunity—while favoring a steadily widening income gap in the name of the free market. This is mere cant and hypocrisy.

In my generation we thought of ourselves as both radical and members of an elite. If this sounds incoherent, it is the incoherence of a certain liberal descent that we intuitively

the birds off the trees": something I attempted fruitlessly in parks for a while before applying the admonition in its Cockney usage to no greater effect during my adolescent years. By then I had graduated from the intensity of polyglot exchanges to the cooler elegance of BBC English.

The 1950s—when I attended elementary school—were a rule-bound age in the teaching and use of the English language. We were instructed in the unacceptability of even the most minor syntactical transgression. "Good" English was at its peak. Thanks to BBC radio and cinema newsreels, there were nationally accepted norms for proper speech; the authority of class and region determined not just how you said things but the kind of things it was appropriate to say. "Accents" abounded (my own included), but were ranked according to respectability: typically a function of social standing and geographical distance from London.

I was seduced by the sheen of English prose at its evanescent apogee. This was the age of mass literacy whose decline Richard Hoggart anticipated in his elegiac essay *The Uses of Literacy* (1957). A literature of protest and revolt was rising through the culture. From *Lucky Jim* through *Look Back in Anger*, and on to the "kitchen sink" dramas of the end of the decade, the class-bound frontiers of suffocating respectability and "proper" speech were under attack. But the barbarians themselves, in their assaults on the heritage, resorted to the perfected cadences of received English: it never occurred to me, reading them, that in order to rebel one must dispense with good form.

By the time I reached college, words were my "thing." As one teacher equivocally observed, I had the talents of a "silver-tongued orator"—combining (as I fondly assured myself) the inherited confidence of the milieu with the critical edge of the outsider. Oxbridge tutorials reward the verbally felicitous student: the neo-Socratic style ("why did you write this?" "what did you mean by it?") invites the solitary recipient to explain himself at length, while implicitly disadvantaging the shy, reflective undergraduate who would prefer to retreat to the back of a seminar. My self-serving faith in articulacy was reinforced: not merely evidence of intelligence but intelligence itself.

Did it occur to me that the silence of the teacher in this pedagogical setting was crucial? Certainly silence was something at which I was never adept, whether as student or teacher. Some of my most impressive colleagues over the years have been withdrawn to the point of inarticulacy in debates and even conversation, thinking with deliberation before committing themselves. I have envied them this self-restraint.

A rticulacy is typically regarded as an aggressive talent. But for me its functions were substantively defensive: rhetorical flexibility allows for a certain feigned closeness—conveying proximity while maintaining distance. That is what actors do—but the world is not really a stage and there is something artificial in the exercise: one sees it in the current US president. I too have marshaled language to fend off intimacy—which perhaps explains a romantic penchant for Protestants and Native Americans, reticent cultures both.

In matters of language, of course, outsiders are frequently deceived: I recall a senior American partner at the consulting firm McKinsey once explaining to me that in the early days of their recruitment in England he found it nearly impossible to choose young associates—everyone seemed so articulate, the analyses tripping off their pens. How could you tell who was smart and who was merely polished?

Words may deceive—mischievous and untrustworthy. I remember being spellbound by the fantasy history of the Soviet Union woven in his Trevelyan Lectures at Cambridge by the elderly Trotskyist Isaac Deutscher (published in 1967 under the title *The Unfinished Revolution: Russia 1917–1967*). The form so elegantly transcended the content that we accepted the latter on trust: detoxification took a while. Sheer rhetorical facility, whatever its appeal, need not denote originality and depth of content.

All the same, *inarticulacy* surely suggests a shortcoming of thought. This idea will sound odd to a generation praised for what they are trying to say rather than the thing said. Articulacy itself became an object of suspicion in the 1970s:

the retreat from "form" favored uncritical approbation of mere "self-expression," above all in the classroom. But it is one thing to encourage students to express their opinions freely and to take care not to crush these under the weight of prematurely imposed authority. It is quite another for teachers to retreat from formal criticism in the hope that the freedom thereby accorded will favor independent thought: "Don't worry how you say it, it's the ideas that count."

Forty years on from the 1960s, there are not many instructors left with the self-confidence (or the training) to pounce on infelicitous expression and explain clearly just why it inhibits intelligent reflection. The revolution of my generation played an important role in this unraveling: the priority accorded the autonomous individual in every sphere of life should not be underestimated—"doing your own thing" took protean form.

Today "natural" expression—in language as in art—is preferred to artifice. We unreflectively suppose that truth no less than beauty is conveyed more effectively thereby. Alexander Pope knew better.[1] For many centuries in the Western tradition, how well you expressed a position corresponded closely to the credibility of your argument. Rhetorical styles might vary from the spartan to the baroque, but style itself was never a matter of indifference. And "style" was not just a well-turned sentence: poor expression belied poor thought. Confused words suggested confused ideas at best, dissimulation at worst.

The "professionalization" of academic writing—and the self-conscious grasping of humanists for the security of "theory" and "methodology"—favors obscurantism. This has encouraged the rise of a counterfeit currency of glib "popular" articulacy: in the discipline of history this is exemplified by the ascent of the "television don," whose appeal lies precisely in his claim to attract a mass audience in an age when fellow scholars have lost interest in communication. But whereas an earlier generation of popular scholarship distilled authorial authority into plain text, today's "accessible" writers protrude uncomfortably into the audience's consciousness. It is the performer, rather than the subject, to whom the audience's attention is drawn.

Cultural insecurity begets its linguistic doppelgänger. The same is true of technical advance. In a world of Facebook, MySpace, and Twitter (not to mention texting), pithy allusion substitutes for exposition. Where once the Internet seemed an opportunity for unrestricted communication, the increasingly commercial bias of the medium—"I am what I buy"—brings impoverishment of its own. My children observe of their own generation that the communicative shorthand of their hardware has begun to seep into communication itself: "people talk like texts."

This ought to worry us. When words lose their integrity so do the ideas they express. If we privilege personal expression over formal convention, then we are privatizing language no less than we have privatized so much else. "When *I* use a word," Humpty Dumpty said, in rather a scornful tone, "it means just what I choose it to mean—neither more nor less." "The question is," said Alice, "whether you *can* make words mean so many different things." Alice was right: the outcome is anarchy.

In "Politics and the English Language," Orwell castigated contemporaries for using language to mystify rather than inform. His critique was directed at bad faith: people wrote poorly because they were trying to say something unclear or else deliberately prevaricating. Our problem, it seems to me, is different. Shoddy prose today bespeaks intellectual insecurity: we speak and write badly because we don't feel confident in what we think and are reluctant to assert it unambiguously ("It's only my opinion . . . "). Rather than suffering from the onset of "newspeak," we risk the rise of "nospeak."

I am more conscious of these considerations now than at any time in the past. In the grip of a neurological disorder, I am fast losing control of words even as my relationship with the world has been reduced to them. They still form with impeccable discipline and unreduced range in the silence of my thoughts—the view from inside is as rich as ever—but I can no longer convey them with ease. Vowel sounds and sibilant consonants slide out of my mouth, shapeless and inchoate even to my close collaborator. The vocal muscle, for sixty years my reliable alter ego, is failing. Communication, performance, assertion: these are now my *weakest* assets. Translating being into thought, thought into words, and words into communication will soon be beyond me and I shall be confined to the rhetorical landscape of my interior reflections.

Though I am now more sympathetic to those constrained to silence I remain contemptuous of garbled language. No longer free to exercise it myself, I appreciate more than ever how vital communication is to the republic: not just the means by which we live together but part of what living together means. The wealth of words in which I was raised were a public space in their own right—and properly preserved public spaces are what we so lack today. If words fall into disrepair, what will substitute? They are all we have.

1. True Wit is Nature to Advantage drest, What oft was Thought, but ne'er so well Exprest. —Alexander Pope, *Essay on Criticism* (1711)

PART THREE

XVIII

Go West, Young Judt

A merica is not everyone's destination of choice.
Few people wake up and say to themselves, "I've
had it with Tajikistan—let's move to America!" After the
war my parents despaired of England (a widespread sentiment in those dreary years); but like so many of their British
contemporaries they looked naturally to the Dominions. In
the high streets of my childhood, grocers and butchers advertised New Zealand lamb and cheese, Australian mutton,
and South African sherry—but American products were
rare. However, plans to settle in New Zealand (and raise
sheep?) were scotched by circumstance and my father's TB
scars. I was duly born in London and was nearly thirty before
my first visit to America.

Everyone thinks they know the United States. What you

"know," of course, depends a lot on how old you are. For elderly Europeans, America is the country that arrived late, rescued them from their history, and irritated with its self-confident prosperity: "What's wrong with the Yanks?" "They're overpaid, oversexed, and over here"—or, in a London variant alluding to cheap ladies' underwear provided under a wartime government scheme: "Have you heard about the new Utility drawers? One Yank and they're off."

For West Europeans raised in the 1950s, "America" was Bing Crosby, Hopalong Cassidy, and overvalued dollars flowing copiously from the plaid pants pockets of midwestern tourists. By the 1970s the image had shifted away from the cowboy West to the Manhattan canyons of Lieutenant Kojak. My generation enthusiastically replaced Bing with Elvis, and Elvis with Motown and the Beach Boys; but we had not the slightest idea what Memphis or Detroit—or southern California for that matter—actually looked like.

America was thus intensely familiar—and completely unknown. Before coming here, I had read Steinbeck, Fitzgerald, and some of the extraordinary short-story writers of the South. Between this and a diet of 1940s-era film noir, I certainly had visual images of the United States. But nothing cohered. Moreover, born like most Europeans in a country I could cross on foot in a matter of days, I had absolutely no grasp of the sheer scale and variety of the place.

I came to the US for the first time in 1975. Upon landing

in Boston, I was supposed to call a Harvard friend with whom we were to stay—but the pay phone required a dime, a coin I could not even identify (Kojak never used them). I was bailed out by a friendly cop, much amused at my ignorance of American coinage.

My English wife and I were planning to drive across the country to Davis, California, where I had been invited to teach for a year. I had thought to buy a used VW Bug, but the first salesman I met talked me into a 1971 Buick LeSabre: gold, automatic, nearly eighteen feet long and capable of ten miles per gallon with a following wind. The first thing we did with the Buick was drive to a pizzeria. In England pizzas were still scarce—and small: a large would have been seven inches across and a half-inch deep. Thus, when the boy behind the counter asked what size, we responded unhesitatingly: "large"—and ordered two of them. We were somewhat nonplussed to be presented with two huge cardboard boxes, each containing a sixteen-inch Chicago-style deep dish meal for ten: my first intimation of the American obsession with size.

Short on funds, we headed west—stopping only to refuel ourselves and the ravenous Buick. The first American motel I ever stayed in was in Sioux Falls, South Dakota. The rates seemed so implausibly low that I tentatively inquired whether we might upgrade to a room with a shower. The desk clerk, after pretending not to understand my accent, explained with undisguised disdain that "all our rooms got showers." To a European ear this was implausible: it was not until we saw it that we actually believed him. Intimation #2: Americans have a thing about clean.

By the time we reached Davis, via Rapid City, South Dakota ("Where the Range War ended") and Reno, we had acquired considerable respect for deep Americana, if not for American cars. This is a "big" country—big sky, big mountains, big fields—and beautiful withal. Even the incontrovertibly ugly aspects are somehow domesticated by their setting: the gas stations and cheap motels that stagger for miles west of Amarillo would spell doom to any European landscape (their Italian counterparts outside Milan are grotesque), but in the greater scheme of West Texas they blend romantically into the evening haze.

Since that first transcontinental drive I have crossed the country seven times. Old established settlements— Cheyenne, Knoxville, Savannah—have continuity on their side. But who could love present-day Houston, Phoenix, or Charlotte? Desolate heaps of office buildings and intersections, they bustle misleadingly from nine to five before dying at dusk. Ozymandias-like, such exurbations will sink back into the marshland or desert whence they arose once the water runs out and gasoline prices them out of existence.

Then there are the ancient coastal settlements, reassuringly grounded in the country's colonial past. Penniless once in New Orleans (mugged in a laundromat), I got an offer to drive a car to Harrisburg, Pennsylvania, for a first-team linebacker of the Pittsburgh Steelers. The vehicle was a long, lean American muscle car, the hood depicting a grinning tiger spread lasciviously across a fur coat. Predictably, we got stopped every fifty miles: the motorcycle cop who pulled us over would swagger up to the window, ready to dress down some overconfident dude in his speeding pimpmobile . . . only to discover a little Cambridge tutor and his terrified wife. After a while we got to enjoying the effect.

Once, in North Platte, Nebraska, I experienced a negative epiphany. In the middle of nowhere, hundreds of miles from anything resembling a city and thousands of miles from the nearest salt water: if *I* felt cut off, surrounded by eight-foot-high fields of corn, what must it be like to live in such a place? No wonder most Americans are profoundly uninterested in what the rest of the world is doing or what it thinks of them. Middle Kingdom? The Chinese didn't know the half of it.

The little towns and settlements dotting the landscape from the Mississippi delta to southern California present a sobering picture. Driving northwest from Dallas toward remotest Decatur on the Texan plateau, each settlement would be represented by a gas station or two, a dowdy (often shuttered) motel, the occasional convenience store, and little clusters of trailer housing. But there was nothing to suggest community.

Except the church. To a European eye, as often as not, it was little more than a warehouse topped by a giant cross.

however, this was a mystery to me: the year completed, I retreated cautiously to the Olde English familiarity of Cambridge. But nothing was quite the same. Cambridge itself felt somehow reduced and constricting: the pancake-flat Fenland as remote as any rice paddy. Everywhere is somewhere else's nowhere.

John Donne describes his mistress as an "America": a new-found-land awaiting erotic discovery. But America herself is a mistress, rebuffing and seducing by turns—even in overweight and boastful middle age she retains a certain allure. For jaded Europeans, the contradictions and curiosities are part of that allure. It is an old-new land engaged in perennial self-discovery (usually at others' expense): an empire sheathed in preindustrial myths, dangerous and innocent.

I was seduced. At first, indecisively, I lurched back and forth across the Atlantic: bestowing my ambivalent affections on both shores. My forebears emigrated of necessity: from fear and destitution. Having no choice, they experienced little doubt. I was a voluntary emigrant and thus could tell myself that my choice was temporary or even revocable. For a long time I toyed with the option of returning to teach in Europe—but it was in America that I felt most European. I was hyphenated: two decades after landing in Boston, I had become an American.

XIX

Midlife Crisis

O ther men change wives. Some change cars. Some change gender. The point of a midlife crisis is to demonstrate continuity with one's youth by doing something strikingly different. To be sure, "different" is a relative term: a man in the throes of such a crisis usually does the same as every other man—that, after all, is how you know it's a midlife crisis. But mine was a little different. I was the right age, at the right stage (divorcing Wife #2), and experiencing the usual middle-aged uncertainties: What's it all about? But I did it my way. I learned Czech.

Early in the 1980s I was teaching politics at Oxford. I had job security, professional responsibilities, and a nice home. Domestic bliss would have been too much to ask, but I was inured to its absence. I did, though, feel increasingly detached from my academic preoccupations. French history in those days had fallen among thieves: the so-called "cultural turn" and "post"-everything trends in social history had me reading interminable turgid screeds, promoted to academic prominence by newly founded "subdisciplines" whose acolytes were starting to colonize a little too close to home. I was bored.

On April 24, 1981, the *New Statesman* carried a letter from a Czech dissident, writing under the pseudonym Václav Racek, politely protesting an essay by E.P. Thompson in which the great British historian had described East and West as coresponsible for the cold war and its attendant crimes. Surely, "Racek" suggested, communism had a little more to answer for? Thompson responded with a long and patronizing dismissal, comparing the Czech dissident's "naive" desire for liberty with his own "defense of British liberties," but conceding that in his misinformed innocence "it is not difficult to understand why a Czech intellectual may think in this way."

I was furious at Thompson's arrogance and wrote in to say so. My intervention—and the sympathies it expressed—elicited an invitation to London to meet Jan Kavan, a '68-era exile. When we met, Kavan was hysterical. He had given an interview to Thames Television in which, carried away by enthusiasm, he had—he feared—inadvertently revealed information about the Czech underground that could get people in trouble. Would I please go and stop the film being shown?

I was flattered that Kavan should suppose an obscure Oxford don capable of wielding such influence. I knew better but pretended otherwise and headed for the studio. The editor of the program listened respectfully to me; quickly ascertained that I knew virtually nothing about Czechoslovakia, the underground opposition, or even Kavan himself; calculated that I was peculiarly without influence even by the standards of my profession . . . and threw me politely out the door.

The film duly ran on television the next night. To my knowledge no one suffered seriously from its revelations, but Jan Kavan's reputation took a severe blow: many years later, when his political enemies in the post-Communist Czech Republic accused him of collaborating with the old regime, the Thames Television interview was invoked as supporting evidence.

As I returned to Oxford that evening, embarrassed by my failure to help and mortified at my own provincialism, I took what would prove, in its small way, to be a decision of consequence. I was going to learn Czech. It was one thing for Thames to ignore me: I did not mind being unimportant. But it offended me to be thought both unimportant and uninformed. For the first time in my life, I had found myself disquisitioning on a place and a problem whose language was unfamiliar to me. I realize that political scientists do this all the time, but that is why I am not a political scientist.

And so, beginning in the early 1980s, I learned a new

language. I began by purchasing *Teach Yourself Czech*. Taking advantage of the lengthy (and increasingly welcome) absences of Wife #2, I devoted two hours a night to this book. Its method was old-fashioned and thus reassuringly familiar: page upon page of grammar, with the emphasis on the complicated conjugations and declensions of the Slavonic family of languages, interspersed with vocabulary, translations, pronunciation, important exceptions, etc. In short, just the way I had been taught German.

After advancing for a few months through this introductory text, I decided that I needed formal instruction if I were to break past the limitations of the isolated autodidact. Oxford in those days offered first-rate language teaching in dozens of familiar and exotic tongues and I duly signed on for a beginner/intermediate-level Czech class. There were only two of us as I recall; my fellow pupil was the wife of a senior Oxford historian and herself a linguist of talent. It took work and concentration to keep up with her.

By the later 1980s I had acquired a passive competence in Czech. I emphasize *passive*: I rarely heard the language spoken outside the audiovisual laboratory, I only visited the country a handful of times, and I was already discovering that—in early middle age—one is slow to master strange tongues. But I could read quite satisfactorily. The first book I read was *Hovory s T.G. Masarykem* (Conversations with Thomas Masaryk) by Karel Capek, a wonderful series of interviews and exchanges between the country's greatest playwright and its first president. From Capek, I advanced to Havel, about whom I started to write.

Learning Czech led me to Czechoslovakia, where I traveled in 1985 and 1986 as a foot soldier in the little army of book smugglers recruited by Roger Scruton to assist lecturers and students expelled from Czech universities or forbidden to attend. I lectured in private apartments to attentive roomfuls of young people, hungry for debate and refreshingly ignorant of academic reputation and fashion. I lectured in English, of course (though older professors would have preferred German). To the extent that I had occasion to use my Czech, it was to respond to unconvincingly casual questions from plainclothes policemen who stood under lampposts outside dissidents' apartments and asked visitors what time it was, to establish whether or not they were foreigners.

Prague in those days was a gray, sad place. Gustáv Husák's Czechoslovakia might have been well-off by Communist standards (second only to Hungary), but it was a grim and depressed land. No one who saw communism in those years could harbor any illusion about the prospects for a dead dogma immured in a decaying society. And yet I spent my days there in a whirl of enthusiasm and excitement, returning to Oxford each time energized and pulsing with ideas.

I began teaching East European history and—with some trepidation—writing it. In particular, I became deeply interested and engaged with the informal, underground opposition there. Reading, discussing, and (eventually) meeting men like Václav Havel, Adam Michnik, János Kis, and their friends, I rediscovered political passions and scholarly and intellectual interests of an urgency unfamiliar—at least to me—since the end of the 1960s . . . and far more serious and consequential than anything I could recall from that decade. It is only a slight exaggeration, and perhaps not even that, to say that my immersion in East-Central Europe brought me back to life.

Back in Oxford, I frequented specialists and refugees from the region. I established programs to host outcast intellectuals from the Soviet bloc. I even began to promote the careers of younger historians and others with an interest in this obscure and absurdly understudied part of Europe—a project I would continue with vastly greater funding after decamping to New York.

Through Poland in particular, and my newfound friends there and in exile, I was able to make links with my own East European Jewish past. Above all, and to my continuing embarrassment, I discovered a rich and seductive literature of which I had been almost completely unaware until then: a shortcoming doubtless attributable to the parochial qualities of even the best British education, but my own responsibility all the same.

Learning Czech, in other words, made me a very different sort of scholar, historian, and person. Would it have made a significant difference had I taken up, say, Polish? My friends certainly thought so: to them, Czech was a *small* Slav lan-

guage (much as Russian colleagues would later describe Polish) and I had inexplicably opted to specialize in what—for
them—was the equivalent of the history of, say, Wales. I felt
otherwise: that distinctly Polish (or Russian) sense of cultural
grandeur was precisely what I wanted to circumnavigate,
preferring the distinctively Czech qualities of doubt, cultural
insecurity, and skeptical self-mockery. These were already
familiar to me from Jewish sources: Kafka, above all—but
Kafka is also the Czech writer par excellence.

Without my Czech obsession I would not have found
myself in Prague in November 1989, watching Havel accept
the presidency from a balcony in the town square. I would
not have sat in the Gellert Hotel in Budapest listening to
János Kis explain his plans for a post-Communist but social
democratic Hungary—the best hope for the region but forlorn even then. I would not have found myself, a few years
later, in the Maramures region of northern Transylvania
making notes for an essay on Romania's post-Communist
traumas.

Above all, I could never have written *Postwar*, my history of Europe since 1945. Whatever its shortcomings, that
book is rare for the determination with which I set out to
integrate Europe's two halves into a common story. In a
way, *Postwar* echoes my own attempt to become an integrated
historian of Europe rather than a disabused critic of French
historical fashion. My Czech adventures did not get me a new
wife (until much later and only indirectly), much less a

new car. But they were the best midlife crisis I could have wished for. They cured me forever of the methodological solipsism of the postmodern academy. They made me, for better or worse, a credible public intellectual. There were more things in heaven and earth than were dreamt of in our Western philosophy and I had—belatedly—seen some of them.

Captive Minds

S ome years ago I visited Krasnogruda, the re-
stored manor house of Czesław Miłosz, close by
the Polish–Lithuanian frontier. I was the guest of Krzysztof
Czyżewski, director of the Borderland Foundation, dedicated
to acknowledging the conflicted memory of this region and
reconciling the local populations. It was deep midwinter
and there were snow-covered fields as far as the eye could
see, with just the occasional clump of ice-bound trees and
posts marking the national frontiers.

My host waxed lyrical over the cultural exchanges
planned for Miłosz's ancestral home. I was absorbed in my
own thoughts: some seventy miles north, in Pilviškiai (Lithuania), the Avigail side of my father's family had lived and

died (some at the hands of the Nazis). Our cousin Meyer London had emigrated in 1891 to New York from a nearby village; there he was elected in 1914 as the second Socialist congressman before being ousted by an ignominious alliance of wealthy New York Jews disturbed by his socialism and American Zionists aghast at his well-publicized suspicion of their project.

For Miłosz, Krasnogruda—"red soil"—was his "native realm" (*Rodzinna Europa* in the original Polish, better translated as European Fatherland or European Family).[1] But for me, staring over this stark white landscape, it stood for Jedwabne, Katyn, and Babi Yar—all within easy reach—not to mention dark memories closer to home. My host certainly knew all this: indeed, he was personally responsible for the controversial Polish publication of Jan Gross's account of the massacre at Jedwabne.[2] But the presence of Poland's greatest twentieth-century poet transcended the tragedy that stalks the region.

Miłosz was born in 1911 in what was then Russian Lithuania. Indeed, like many great Polish literary figures, he was not strictly "Polish" by geographical measure. Adam Zagajewski, one of the country's most important living poets, was born in Ukraine; Jerzy Giedroyc—a major figure in the twentieth-century literary exile—was born in Belarus, like Adam Mickiewicz, the nineteenth-century icon of the Polish literary revival. Lithuanian Vilna in particular was a cosmopolitan blend of Poles, Lithuanians, Germans, Russians, and Jews, among others (Isaiah Berlin, like the Harvard political philosopher Judith Shklar, was born in nearby Riga).

Raised in the interwar Polish republic, Miłosz survived the occupation and was already a poet of some standing when he was sent to Paris as the cultural attaché of the new People's Republic. But in 1951 he defected to the West and two years later he published his most influential work, *The Captive Mind*.[3] Never out of print, it is by far the most insightful and enduring account of the attraction of intellectuals to Stalinism and, more generally, of the appeal of authority and authoritarianism to the intelligentsia.

Miłosz studies four of his contemporaries and the self-delusions to which they fell prey on their journey from autonomy to obedience, emphasizing what he calls the intellectuals' need for "a feeling of belonging." Two of his subjects—Jerzy Andrzejewski and Tadeusz Borowski—may be familiar to English readers, Andrzejewski as the author of *Ashes and Diamonds* (adapted for the cinema by Andrzej Wajda) and Borowski as the author of a searing memoir of Auschwitz, *This Way for the Gas, Ladies and Gentlemen*.

But the book is most memorable for two images. One is the "Pill of Murti-Bing." Miłosz came across this in an obscure novel by Stanisław Ignacy Witkiewicz, *Insatiability* (1927). In this story, Central Europeans facing the prospect of being overrun by unidentified Asiatic hordes pop a little pill, which relieves them of fear and anxiety; buoyed by its effects, they not only accept their new rulers but are positively happy to receive them.

The second image is that of "Ketman," borrowed from Arthur de Gobineau's *Religions and Philosophies of Central Asia*, in which the French traveler reports the Persian phenomenon of elective identities. Those who have internalized the way of being called "Ketman" can live with the contradictions of saying one thing and believing another, adapting freely to each new requirement of their rulers while believing that they have preserved somewhere within themselves the autonomy of a free thinker—or at any rate a thinker who has freely chosen to subordinate himself to the ideas and dictates of others.

Ketman, in Miłosz's words, "brings comfort, fostering dreams of what might be, and even the enclosing fence affords the solace of reverie." Writing for the desk drawer becomes a sign of inner liberty. At least his audience *would* take him seriously if only they could read him.

Fear of the indifference with which the economic system of the West treats its artists and scholars is widespread among Eastern intellectuals. They say it is better to deal with an intelligent devil than with a good-natured idiot.

Between Ketman and the Pill of Murti-Bing, Miłosz brilliantly dissects the state of mind of the fellow traveler, the deluded idealist, and the cynical time server. His essay is more subtle than Arthur Koestler's *Darkness at Noon* and less relentlessly logical than Raymond Aron's *Opium of the Intellectuals*. I used to teach it in what was for many years my favorite course, a survey of essays and novels from Central and Eastern Europe that included the writings of Milan Kundera, Václav Havel, Ivo Andrić, Heda Kovály, Paul Goma, and others.

But I began to notice that whereas the novels of Kundera and Andrić, or the memoirs of Kovaly or Yevgenia Ginsburg, remain accessible to American students notwithstanding the alien material, *The Captive Mind* often encountered incomprehension. Miłosz takes for granted his readers' intuitive grasp of the believer's state of mind: the man or woman who has identified with History and enthusiastically aligned themselves with a system that denies them freedom of expression. In 1951 he could reasonably assume that this phenomenon—whether associated with communism, fascism, or indeed any other form of political repression—would be familiar.

And indeed, when I first taught the book in the 1970s, I spent most of my time explaining to would-be radical students just why a "captive mind" was not a good thing. Thirty years on, my young audience is simply mystified: why would someone sell his soul to *any* idea, much less a repressive one? By the turn of the twenty-first century, few of my North American students had ever met a Marxist. A self-abnegating commitment to a secular faith was beyond their imaginative reach. When I started out my challenge was to explain why people became disillusioned with Marxism; today, the insuperable hurdle one faces is explaining the illusion itself.

Contemporary students do not see the point of the book: the whole exercise seems futile. Repression, suffering, irony, and even religious belief: these they can grasp. But ideological self-delusion? Miłosz's posthumous readers thus resemble the Westerners and émigrés whose incomprehension he describes so well: "They do not know how one pays—those abroad do not know. They do not know what one buys, and at what price."

Perhaps so. But there is more than one kind of captivity. Recall the Ketman-like trance of those intellectuals swept up in George W. Bush's hysterical drive to war just a few years ago. Few of them would have admitted to admiring the President, much less sharing his worldview. So they typically aligned themselves behind him while doubtless maintaining private reservations. Later, when it was clear they had made a mistake, they blamed it upon the administration's incompetence. With Ketman-like qualifications they proudly assert, in effect, "we were right to be wrong"—a revealing if unconscious echo of the *plaidoyer* of the French fellow travelers, "better to have been wrong with Sartre than right with Aron."

Today, we can still hear sputtering echoes of the attempt to reignite the cold war around a crusade against "Islamo-fascism." But the true mental captivity of our time lies else-where. Our contemporary faith in "the market" rigorously tracks its radical nineteenth-century doppelgänger—the un-questioning belief in necessity, progress, and History. Just as the hapless British Labour chancellor in 1929–1931, Philip Snowden, threw up his hands in the face of the Depression and declared that there was no point opposing the ineluctable laws of capitalism, so Europe's leaders today scuttle into budgetary austerity to appease "the markets."

But "the market"—like "dialectical materialism"—is just an abstraction: at once ultra-rational (its argument trumps all) and the acme of unreason (it is not open to question). It has its true believers—mediocre thinkers by contrast with the founding fathers, but influential withal; its fellow travelers—who may privately doubt the claims of the dogma but see no alternative to preaching it; and its victims, many of whom in the US especially have dutifully swallowed their pill and proudly proclaim the virtues of a doctrine whose benefits they will never see.

Above all, the thrall in which an ideology holds a people is best measured by their collective inability to imagine alter-natives. We know perfectly well that untrammeled faith in unregulated markets kills: the rigid application of what was until recently the "Washington consensus" in vulnerable de-veloping countries—with its emphasis on tight fiscal policy, privatization, low tariffs, and deregulation—has destroyed millions of livelihoods. Meanwhile, the stringent "commercial terms" on which vital pharmaceuticals are made available has drastically reduced life expectancy in many places. But in Margaret Thatcher's deathless phrase, "there is no alternative."

It was in just such terms that communism was presented to its beneficiaries following World War II; and it was because History afforded no apparent alternative to a Communist future that so many of Stalin's foreign admirers were swept into intellectual captivity. But when Miłosz published *The Captive Mind*, Western intellectuals were still debating among genuinely competitive social models—whether social democratic, social market, or regulated market variants of liberal capitalism. Today, despite the odd Keynesian protest from below the salt, a consensus reigns.

For Miłosz, "the man of the East cannot take Americans seriously because they have never undergone the experiences that teach men how relative their judgments and thinking habits are." This is doubtless so and explains the continuing skepticism of the East European in the face of Western innocence. But there is nothing innocent about Western (and Eastern) commentators' voluntary servitude before the new pan-orthodoxy. Many of them, Ketman-like, know better but prefer not to raise their heads above the parapet. In this sense at least, they have something truly in common with the intellectuals of the Communist age. One hundred years after his birth, fifty-seven years after the publication of his seminal essay, Miłosz's indictment of the servile intellectual rings truer than ever: "his chief characteristic is his fear of thinking for himself."

1. Czesław Miłosz, *Native Realm* (*Rodzinna Europa*) (1959; Doubleday, 1968).
2. Jan Gross, *Neighbors: The Destruction of the Jewish Community in Jedwabne, Poland* (Princeton University Press, 2001).
3. Czesław Miłosz, *The Captive Mind* (*Zniewolony umysł*) (1953; Vintage, 1981).

XXI

Girls, Girls, Girls

In 1992 I was chairman of the History Department at New York University—where I was also the only unmarried straight male under sixty. A combustible blend: prominently displayed on the board outside my office was the location and phone number of the university's Sexual Harassment Center. History was a fast-feminizing profession, with a graduate community primed for signs of discrimination— or worse. Physical contact constituted a presumption of malevolent intention; a closed door was proof positive.

Shortly after I took office, a second-year graduate student came by. A former professional ballerina interested in Eastern Europe, she had been encouraged to work with me. I was not teaching that semester, so could have advised her to return another time. Instead, I invited her in. After a closed-door discussion of Hungarian economic reforms, I suggested a course of independent study—beginning the following evening at a local restaurant. A few sessions later, in a fit of bravado, I invited her to the premiere of *Oleanna*—David Mamet's lame dramatization of sexual harassment on a college campus.

How to explain such self-destructive behavior? What delusional universe was mine, to suppose that I alone could pass untouched by the punitive prudery of the hour—that the bell of sexual correctness would not toll for me? I knew my Foucault as well as anyone and was familiar with Firestone, Millett, Brownmiller, Faludi, *e tutte quante*.[1] To say that the girl had irresistible eyes and that my intentions were . . . unclear would avail me nothing. My excuse? *Please Sir, I'm from the '60s.*

The life of an early-'60s adolescent male was curiously confined. We still inhabited our parents' moral universe. Dating was difficult—no one had cars; our homes were too small for privacy; contraception was available but only if you were willing to confront a disapproving pharmacist. There was a well-founded presumption of innocence and ignorance, for boys and girls alike. Most boys I knew attended single-sex schools and we rarely encountered women. A friend and I paid hard-earned money for Saturday morning dance classes at the Locarno Ballroom in Streatham; but when it came time for the annual social, the girls from

Godolphin & Latymer School laughed at us all the same. We cut the experiment short.

Even if you got a date, it was like courting your grandmother. Girls in those days came buttressed in an impenetrable Maginot Line of hooks, belts, girdles, nylons, roll-ons, suspenders, slips, and petticoats. Older boys assured me that these were mere erotic impedimenta, easily circumnavigated. I found them terrifying. And I was not alone, as any number of films and novels from that era can illustrate. Back then we all lived on Chesil Beach.

A nd then, to our surprise, we learned that we were part of the "sexual revolution." Within a matter of months, a generation of young women abandoned a century of lingerie and adopted the miniskirt with (or without) tights. Few men of my acquaintance born later than 1952 have even heard of—much less encountered—most of the undergarments listed above. The French pop star Antoine sang optimistically of buying contraceptive pills in the Monoprix (approximately France's K-Mart).[2] At Cambridge, cool and worldly, I helped a friend arrange an abortion for his girl. Everyone was "playing with fire."

Or claiming to. My generation was obsessed with the distinction between theory and practice—I knew a man in California whose doctoral dissertation was devoted to "Theory and Practice in theory and in practice." Sexually, we lived the contrast. In *theory* we prided ourselves on being the cutting edge. But in *practice* we were a conformist co-hort: shaped more by our '50s youth than our '60s adolescence. A surprising number of us married young—often to our first serious girlfriend. And of that number, many have stayed married. Championing the inalienable right of everyone to do anything, we had scant occasion to do much ourselves.

Our predecessors had grown up in the claustrophobic world of *Lucky Jim* and *Look Back in Anger*. Constrained by the limits they were taught to respect, they might try to seduce an office junior or a female student but were instinctively rule-bound: they did not expect to live out their fantasies. We, by contrast, had trouble distinguishing our fantasies from everyday life. The solipsism of the '60s— "make love, not war," "do your own thing," "let it all hang out"—certainly destroyed taboos. But it also muffled the conscience: nothing was off-limits.

In 1981, shortly after arriving at Oxford, I invited a student and her boyfriend to dinner. My wife and I lived in a country village and by the time the young couple arrived it was snowing hard. They would have to stay overnight. I casually pointed out the tiny guestroom with its double bed and wished them good night. Only much later did it occur to me to wonder whether the pair were sleeping together. When I delicately alluded to the matter a few days later, the young woman patted me on the shoulder: "Don't worry Tony, we understood. You '60s types!"

Our successors—liberated from old-style constraints—have imposed new restrictions upon themselves. Since the 1970s, Americans assiduously avoid anything that might smack of harassment, even at the risk of forgoing promising friendships and the joys of flirtation. Like men of an earlier decade—though for very different reasons—they are preternaturally wary of missteps. I find this depressing. The Puritans had a sound theological basis for restricting their desires and those of others. But today's conformists have no such story to tell.

Nevertheless, the anxieties of contemporary sexual relations offer occasional comic relief. When I was Humanities dean at NYU, a promising young professor was accused of improper advances by a graduate student in his department. He had apparently followed her into a supply closet and declared his feelings. Confronted, the professor confessed all, begging me not to tell his wife. My sympathies were divided: the young man had behaved foolishly, but there was no question of intimidation nor had he offered to trade grades for favors. All the same, he was censured. Indeed, his career was ruined—the department later denied him tenure because no women would take his courses. Meanwhile, his "victim" was offered the usual counseling.

Some years later, I was called to the Office of the University Lawyer. Would I serve as a witness for the defense in a case against NYU being brought by that same young woman? Note, the lawyer warned me: "she" is really a "he" and is suing the university for failing to take seriously "her" needs as a transvestite. We shall fight the case but must not be thought insensitive.

So I appeared in Manhattan Supreme Court to explain the complexities of academic harassment to a bemused jury of plumbers and housewives. The student's lawyer pressed hard: "Were you not prejudiced against my client because of her transgendered identity preference?" "I don't see how I could have been," I replied. "I thought she was a woman—isn't that what she wanted me to think?" The university won the case.

On another occasion, a student complained that I "discriminated" against her because she did not offer sexual favors. When the department *ombudswoman*—a sensible lady of impeccable radical credentials—investigated, it emerged that the complainant resented not being invited to join my seminar: she assumed that women who took part must be getting (and offering) favorable treatment. I explained that it was because they were smarter. The young woman was flabbergasted: the only form of discrimination she could imagine was sexual. It had never occurred to her that I might just be an elitist.

This story is revealing. When discussing sexually explicit literature—Milan Kundera, to take an obvious case—with European students, I have always found them comfortable debating the topic. Conversely, young Americans of both sexes—usually so forthcoming— fall nervously silent: reluctant to engage the subject lest they transgress boundaries. Yet sex—or, to adopt the term of art, "gender"—is the first thing that comes to mind when they try to explain the behavior of adults in the real world.

Here as in so many other arenas, we have taken the '60s altogether too seriously. Sexuality (or gender) is just as distorting when we fixate upon it as when we deny it. Substituting gender (or "race" or "ethnicity" or "me") for social class or income category could only have occurred to people for whom politics was a recreational avocation, a projection of self onto the world at large.

Why should everything be about "me"? Are my fixations of significance to the Republic? Do my particular needs by definition speak to broader concerns? What on earth does it mean to say that "the personal is political"? If everything is "political," then nothing is. I am reminded of Gertrude Stein's Oxford lecture on contemporary literature. "What about the woman question?" someone asked. Stein's reply should be emblazoned on every college notice board from Boston to Berkeley: "Not everything can be about everything."

The playful mantras of our adolescence have become a way of life for later generations. At least in the '60s we knew, whatever we said, that sex was about . . . sex. All the same, what followed is our fault. We—the left, academics, teachers—have abandoned politics to those for whom actual power is far more interesting than its metaphorical implications. Political correctness, gender politics, and above all hypersensitivity to wounded sentiments (as though there were a right not to be offended): this will be our legacy.

Why should I not close my office door or take a student to a play? If I hesitate, have I not internalized the worst sort of communitarian self-censorship—anticipating my own guilt long before I am accused and setting a pusillanimous example for others? Yes: and if only for these reasons I see nothing wrong in my behavior. But were it not for the mandarin self-assurance of my Oxbridge years, I too might lack the courage of my convictions—though I readily concede that the volatile mix of intellectual arrogance and generational exceptionalism can ignite delusions of invulnerability.

Indeed, it is just such a sense of boundless entitlement—taken to extremes—that helps explain Bill Clinton's self-destructive transgressions or Tony Blair's insistence that he was right to lie his way into a war whose necessity he alone could assess. But note that for all their brazen philandering and posturing, Clinton and Blair—no less than Bush, Gore,

Brown, and so many others of my generation—are still married to their first serious date. I cannot claim as much—I was divorced in 1977 and again in 1986—but in other respects the curious '60s blend of radical attitudes and domestic convention ensnared me too. So how did I elude the harassment police, who surely were on my tail as I surreptitiously dated my bright-eyed ballerina?

Reader: I married her.

1. Authors, respectively, of *The Dialectic of Sex*, *Sexual Politics*, *Against Our Will* and *Backlash: The Undeclared War Against American Women*.
2. "Comment faire pour enrichir le pays?
Mettez la pillule en vente dans les Monoprix." *Élucubrations*, 1966.

XXII

New York, New York

I came to New York University in 1987 on a whim. The Thatcherite assault on British higher education was just beginning and even in Oxford the prospects were grim. NYU appealed to me: by no means a recent foundation—it was established in 1831—it is nevertheless the junior of New York City's great universities. Less of a "city on a hill," it is more open to new directions: in contrast to the cloistered collegiate worlds of Oxbridge, it brazenly advertises itself as a "global" university at the heart of a world city.

But just what is a "world city"? Mexico City, at eighteen million people, or São Paolo at one million less, are unmanageable urban sprawls; but they are not "world cities." Conversely, Paris—whose central districts have never exceeded two million inhabitants—was "the capital of the nineteenth century." Is it a function of the number of visitors? In that case, Orlando (Florida) would be a great metropolis. Being the capital of a country guarantees nothing: think of Madrid or Washington, DC (the Brasilia of its time). It may not even be a matter of wealth: within the foreseeable future Shanghai (fourteen million people) and Singapore (five million people) will surely be among the richest places on earth. Will they be "world cities"?

I have lived in four such cities. London was the commercial and financial center of the world from the defeat of Napoleon until the rise of Hitler; Paris—its perennial competitor—was an international cultural magnet from the building of Versailles through the death of Albert Camus. Vienna's apogee was perhaps the shortest: its rise and fall coincided with the last years of the Habsburg Empire, though in intensity it outshone them all. And then came New York.

It has been my mixed fortune to experience these cities at twilight. In their prime they were arrogant and self-assured. In decline, their minor virtues come into focus: people spend less time telling you how fortunate you are to be there. Even at the height of "Swinging London" there was something brittle about the city's self-promotion, as though it knew this was but an Indian summer.

Today, the British capital is doubtless geographically central—its awful bling-bloated airport the world's busiest. And the city can boast the best theatre and a multicolored cosmopolitanism sadly lacking in years past. But it all rests precariously upon an unsustainable heap of other peoples' money: the capital of capital.

By the time I got to Paris, most people in the world had stopped speaking French (something the French have been slow to acknowledge). Who now would deliberately reconstruct their city—as the Romanians did in the late nineteenth century—in order to become "the Paris of the East," complete with *grands boulevards* like the Calea Victoria? The French have a word for the disposition to look insecurely inwards, to be preoccupied with self-interrogation: *nombrilisme* "navel gazing." They have been doing it for over a century.

I arrived in New York just in time to experience the bittersweet taste of loss. In the arts the city led the world from 1945 through the 1970s. If you wanted to see modern painting, experience music, or dance, you came to the New York of Clement Greenberg, Leonard Bernstein, and George Balanchine. Culture was more than an object of consumption: people thronged to New York to produce it too. Manhattan in those decades was the crossroads where interesting and original minds lingered—drawing others in their wake. Nothing else came close.

Jewish New York too is past its peak. Who now cares what *Dissent* or (particularly) *Commentary* say to the world or one another? In 1979 Woody Allen could count on a wide audience for a joke about the two of them merging and forming "Dissentary" (see *Annie Hall*). Today? A disproportionate amount of the energy invested in these and certain other small journals goes to the "Israel" question: perhaps the closest that Americans get to *nombrilisme*.

The intellectual gangs of New York have folded their knives and gone home to the suburbs—or else they fight it out in academic departments to the utter indifference of the rest of humanity. The same, of course, is true of the self-referential squabbles of the cultural elites of Russia or Argentina. But that is one reason why neither Moscow nor Buenos Aires matters on the world stage. New York intellectuals once did, but most of them have gone the way of Viennese café society: they have become a parody of themselves, their institutions and controversies of predominantly local concern.

And yet New York *remains* a world city. It is not the great American city—that will always be Chicago. New York sits at the edge: like Istanbul or Mumbai, its distinctive appeal lies precisely in its cantankerous relationship to the metropolitan territory beyond. It looks *outward*, and is thus attractive to people who would not feel comfortable further inland. It has never been American in the way that Paris is French: New York has always been about something else as well.

Shortly after arriving here, I wandered into a local tailor's shop to get something altered. After measuring me, the elderly owner glanced up: "Ver you tek your laundry?" "Well," I responded, "to the Chinese laundry at the corner." He rose and gave me a long, hard look, peeling away layers of Paris, Cambridge, south London, Antwerp, and points east: "Vy you teking the laundry to the Chinaman?"

Today I drop my cleaning off with Joseph the tailor and we exchange Yiddishisms and reminiscences (his) of Jewish Russia. Two blocks south I lunch at Bar Pitti, whose Florentine owner disdains credit cards and prepares the best Tuscan food in New York. In a hurry, I can opt instead for a falafel from the Israelis on the next block; I might do even better with the sizzling lamb from the Arab at the corner.

Fifty meters away are my barbers: Giuseppe, Franco, and Salvatore, all from Sicily—their "English" echoing Chico Marx. They have been in Greenwich Village forever but never really settled: how should they? They shout at one another all day in Sicilian dialect, drowning out their main source of entertainment and information: a twenty-four hour Italian-language radio station. On my way home, I enjoy a *millefeuilles* from Claude: a surly Breton *pâtissier* who has put his daughter through the London School of Economics, one exquisite éclair at a time.

All this within two square blocks of my apartment—and I am neglecting the Sikh newsstand, the Hungarian bakery, and the Greek diner (actually Albanian but we pretend otherwise). Three streets east and I have Little Habsburgia: Ukrainian restaurant, Uniate church, Polish grocery, and, of course, the long-established Jewish deli—serving East European staples under kosher labels. All that is missing is a

Viennese café—for this, symptomatically, you must go up-town to the wealthy quarters of the city.

Such variety is doubtless available in London. But the cultures of contemporary London are balkanized by district and income—Canary Wharf, the financial hub, keeps its distance from the ethnic enclaves at the center. Contrast Wall Street, within easy walking distance of my neighborhood. As for Paris, it has its sequestered quarters where the grandchildren of Algerian guest workers rub shoulders with Senegalese street vendors; Amsterdam its Surinamese and Indonesian districts: but these are the backwash of empire, what Europeans now refer to as the "immigrant question."

One must not romanticize. I am sure most of my neighborhood traders and artisans have never met and would have little to say to one another: at night they return home to Queens or New Jersey. If I told Joseph or Sal they had the good fortune to live in a "world city," they would probably snort. But they do—just as the barrow boys of early twentieth-century Hoxton were citizens of the same cosmopolitan London that Keynes memorialized in *The Economic Consequences of the Peace*, even though they would have had no idea what he was talking about.

At a dinner party here in NYC, I was once asked what I thought were America's three strongest assets. I replied without hesitation: "Thomas Jefferson, Chuck Berry, and the *New York Review of Books*." To avoid being forced to rank them, I also invoked the glories of the Fifth Amendment. I was not joking. Thomas Jefferson requires no explanation (though in the current atmosphere of textbook censorship, he could use some defense). Chuck Berry requires no apology. But the city's enduring international influence is perfectly encapsulated in the *NYRB*: perhaps the last survivor (founded in 1963) of New York's halcyon era.

It is no accident that today we have a London Review of Books, a Budapest Review of Books, an Athens Review of Books, a proposal for a European Review of Books, and even a Jewish Review of Books: each in its way a nod to the influence of the homonymic model. And yet they fall short. Why? The London Review of Books is exemplary in its way (though I should recuse myself here as an occasional contributor); but it is distinctly a *London* product, reflecting a metropolitan leftism that is unmistakably English if not Oxbridge. The others are overtly partisan and parochial. In Budapest, my commissioned essay on the Hungarian writer György Konrád was spiked for *lèse-majesté*; attempts to found a "Paris Review of Books" have foundered on the local assumption that it must serve as a platform for publishers' puffs and the exchange of literary favors.

What distinguishes the *New York Review*[1] is precisely that it is not about New York—nor is it written primarily by New Yorkers: like the city itself, it is tangential to its point of origin. If this is a world city, it is not thanks to the Ukrainian restaurants on 2nd Avenue, nor even the Ukrainians who have colonized Brighton Beach: they can be found in many other places from Cleveland to Chicago. It is that cultivated Ukrainians in *Kiev* read New York's best-known periodical.

We are experiencing the decline of the American age. But how does national or imperial decay influence the life cycle of a world city? Modern-day Berlin is a cultural metropolis on the make, despite being the capital of a medium-sized and rather self-absorbed nation. As for Paris, we have seen that it retained its allure for nearly two centuries after the onset of French national decline.

New York—a city more at home in the world than in its home country—may do better still. As a European, I feel more myself in New York than in the EU's semi-detached British satellite: and I have Brazilian and Arab friends here who share the sentiment. To be sure, we all have our complaints. And while there is no other city where I could imagine living, there are many places that, for different purposes, I would rather be. But this too is a very New York sentiment. Chance made me an American, but I chose to be a New Yorker. I probably always was.

1 Full disclosure: I occasionally publish there.

XXIII

Edge People

I dentity" is a dangerous word. It has no respectable contemporary uses. In Britain, the mandarins of New Labour—not satisfied with installing more closed-circuit surveillance cameras than any other democracy—have sought (so far unsuccessfully) to invoke the "war on terror" as an occasion to introduce mandatory identity cards. In France and the Netherlands, artificially stimulated "national debates" on identity are a flimsy cover for political exploitation of anti-immigrant sentiment—and a blatant ploy to deflect economic anxiety onto minority targets. In Italy, the politics of identity were reduced in December 2009 to house-to-house searches in the Brescia region for unwanted dark faces as the municipality shamelessly promised a "white Christmas."

In academic life, the word has comparably mischievous uses. Undergraduates today can select from a swathe of identity studies: "gender studies," "women's studies," "Asian-Pacific-American studies," and dozens of others. The shortcoming of all these para-academic programs is not that they concentrate on a given ethnic or geographical minority; it is that they encourage members of that minority to study *themselves*—thereby simultaneously negating the goals of a liberal education and reinforcing the sectarian and ghetto mentalities they purport to undermine. All too frequently, such programs are job-creation schemes for their incumbents, and outside interest is actively discouraged. Blacks study blacks, gays study gays, and so forth.

As so often, academic taste follows fashion. These programs are byproducts of communitarian solipsism: today we are all hyphenated—Irish-Americans, Native Americans, African-Americans, and the like. Most people no longer speak the language of their forebears or know much about their country of origin, especially if their family started out in Europe. But in the wake of a generation of boastful victim-hood, they wear what little they do know as a proud badge of identity: you are what your grandparents suffered. In this competition, Jews stand out. Many American Jews are sadly ignorant of their religion, culture, traditional languages, or history. But they do know about Auschwitz, and that suffices.

This warm bath of identity was always alien to me. I grew up in England and English is the language in which I think and write. London—my birthplace— remains familiar to me for all the many changes that it has seen over the decades. I know the country well; I even share some of its prejudices and predilections. But when I think or speak of the English, I instinctively use the third person: I don't *identify* with them.

In part this may be because I am Jewish; when I was growing up Jews were the only significant minority in Christian Britain and the object of mild but unmistakable cultural prejudice. On the other hand, my parents stood quite apart from the organized Jewish community. We celebrated no Jewish holidays (I always had a Christmas tree and Easter eggs), followed no rabbinical injunctions, and only identified with Judaism over Friday evening meals with grandparents. Thanks to an English schooling, I am more familiar with the Anglican liturgy than with many of the rites and practices of Judaism. So if I grew up Jewish, it was as a decidedly non-Jewish Jew.

Did this tangential relationship to Englishness derive from my father's birthplace (Antwerp)? Possibly, but then he too lacked a conventional "identity": he was not a Belgian citizen but the child of stateless migrants who had come to

Antwerp from the tsarist empire. Today we would say his parents were born in what had not yet become Poland and Lithuania. However, neither of these newly formed countries would have given the time of day—much less citizenship— to a pair of Belgian Jews. And even though my mother (like me) was born in the East End of London, and was thus a genuine Cockney, her parents came from Russia and Romania: countries of which she knew nothing and whose languages she could not speak. Like hundreds of thousands of Jewish immigrants, they communicated in Yiddish, a language that was of no discernible service to their children.

I was thus neither English nor Jewish. And yet, I feel strongly that I am—in different ways and at different times— both. Perhaps such genetic identifications are less consequential than we suppose? What of the elective affinities I acquired over the years: am I a French historian? I certainly studied the history of France and speak the language well; but unlike most of my fellow Anglo-Saxon students of France, I never fell in love with Paris and have always felt ambivalent about it. I have been accused of thinking and even writing like a French intellectual—a barbed compliment. But French intellectuals, with outstanding exceptions, leave me cold: theirs is a club from which I would happily be excluded.

What of *political* identity? As the child of self-taught Jews brought up in the shadow of the Russian Revolution, I acquired from an early age a superficial familiarity with Marxist texts and socialist history—enough to inoculate me against the wilder strains of 1960s-era New Leftism while leaving me firmly in the social democratic camp. Today, as a "public intellectual" (itself an unhelpful label), I am associated with whatever remains of the left.

But within the university, many colleagues look upon me as a reactionary dinosaur. Understandably so: I teach the textual legacy of long-dead Europeans; have little tolerance for "self-expression" as a substitute for clarity; regard effort as a poor substitute for achievement; treat my discipline as dependent in the first instance upon facts, not "theory"; and view with skepticism much that passes for historical scholarship today. By prevailing academic mores, I am incorrigibly conservative. So which is it?

As an English-born student of European history teaching in the US; as a Jew somewhat uncomfortable with much that passes for "Jewishness" in contemporary America; as a social democrat frequently at odds with my self-described radical colleagues, I suppose I should seek comfort in the familiar insult of "rootless cosmopolitan." But that seems to me too imprecise, too deliberately universal in its ambitions. Far from being rootless, I am all too well rooted in a variety of contrasting heritages.

In any event, all such labels make me uneasy. We know enough of ideological and political movements to be wary of exclusive solidarity in all its forms. One should keep one's distance not only from the obviously unappealing "-isms"— fascism, jingoism, chauvinism—but also from the more seductive variety: communism, to be sure, but nationalism and Zionism too. And then there is national pride: more than two centuries after Samuel Johnson first made the point, patriotism—as anyone who passed the last decade in America can testify—is still the last refuge of the scoundrel.

I prefer the edge: the place where countries, communities, allegiances, affinities, and roots bump uncomfortably up against one another—where cosmopolitanism is not so much an identity as the normal condition of life. Such places once abounded. Well into the twentieth century there were many cities comprising multiple communities and languages—often mutually antagonistic, occasionally clashing, but somehow coexisting. Sarajevo was one, Alexandria another. Tangiers, Salonica, Odessa, Beirut, and Istanbul all qualified—as did smaller towns like Chernovitz and Uzhhorod. By the standards of American conformism, New York resembles aspects of these lost cosmopolitan cities: that is why I live here.

To be sure, there is something self-indulgent in the assertion that one is always at the edge, on the margin. Such a claim is only open to a certain kind of person exercising very particular privileges. Most people, most of the time, would rather *not* stand out: it is not safe. If everyone else is a Shia, better to be a Shia. If everyone in Denmark is tall and white, then who—given a choice—would opt to be short and brown? And even in an open democracy, it takes a certain obstinacy of character to work willfully against the grain of one's community, especially if it is small.

But if you are born at intersecting margins and—thanks to the peculiar institution of academic tenure— are at liberty to remain there, it seems to me a decidedly advantageous perch: What should they know of England, who only England know? If identification with a community of origin was fundamental to my sense of self, I would perhaps hesitate before criticizing Israel—the "Jewish State," "my people"—so roundly. Intellectuals with a more developed sense of organic affiliation instinctively self-censor: they think twice before washing dirty linen in public.

Unlike the late Edward Said, I believe I can understand and even empathize with those who know what it means to love a country. I don't regard such sentiments as incomprehensible; I just don't share them. But over the years these fierce unconditional loyalties—to a country, a God, an idea, or a man—have come to terrify me. The thin veneer of civilization rests upon what may well be an illusory faith in our common humanity. But illusory or not, we would do well to cling to it. Certainly, it is that faith—and the constraints it places upon human misbehavior—that is the first to go in times of war or civil unrest.

We are entering, I suspect, upon a time of troubles. It is not just the terrorists, the bankers, and the climate that are going to wreak havoc with our sense of security and stability. Globalization itself—the "flat" earth of so many irenic fantasies—will be a source of fear and uncertainty to billions of people who will turn to their leaders for protection. "Identities" will grow mean and tight, as the indigent and the uprooted beat upon the ever-rising walls of gated communities from Delhi to Dallas.

Being "Danish" or "Italian," "American" or "European" won't just be an identity; it will be a rebuff and a reproof to those whom it excludes. The state, far from disappearing, may be about to come into its own: the privileges of citizenship, the protections of card-holding residency rights, will be wielded as political trumps. Intolerant demagogues in established democracies will demand "tests"—of knowledge, of language, of attitude—to determine whether desperate newcomers are deserving of British or Dutch or French "identity." They are already doing so. In this brave new century we shall miss the tolerant, the marginals: the edge people. My people.

XXIV

Toni

I never knew Toni Avegael. She was born in Antwerp in February 1926 and lived there most of her life. We were related: she was my father's first cousin. I well remember her older sister Lily: a tall, sad lady whom my parents and I used to visit in a little house somewhere in northwest London. We have long since lost touch, which is a pity.

I am reminded of the Avegael sisters (there was a middle girl, Bella) whenever I ask myself—or am asked—what it means to be Jewish. There is no general-purpose answer to this question: it is always a matter of what it means to be Jewish for me—something quite distinct from what it means for my fellow Jews. To outsiders, such concerns are mysterious. A Protestant who does not believe in the Scriptures, a Catholic who abjures the authority of the Pope in Rome, or a Muslim for whom Muhammad is not the Prophet: these are incoherent categories. But a Jew who rejects the authority of the rabbis is still Jewish (even if only by the rabbis' own matrilineal definition): who is to tell him otherwise?

I reject the authority of the rabbis—all of them (and for this I have rabbinical authority on my side). I participate in no Jewish community life, nor do I practice Jewish rituals. I don't make a point of socializing with Jews in particular—and for the most part I haven't married them. I am not a "lapsed" Jew, having never conformed to requirements in the first place. I don't "love Israel" (either in the modern sense or in the original generic meaning of loving the Jewish people), and I don't care if the sentiment is reciprocated. But whenever anyone asks me whether or not I am Jewish, I unhesitatingly respond in the affirmative and would be ashamed to do otherwise.

The ostensible paradox of this condition is clearer to me since coming to New York: the curiosities of Jewish identity are more salient here. Most American Jews of my acquaintance are not particularly well informed about Jewish culture or history; they are blithely ignorant of Yiddish or Hebrew and rarely attend religious ceremonies. When they do, they behave in ways that strike me as curious.

Shortly after arriving in New York, I was invited to a bar mitzvah. On my way to the synagogue, I realized I had forgotten my hat and returned home to recover it—only to observe that almost no one else covered his head during the brief, exiguous excuse for a religious ceremony. To be sure, this was a "Reform" synagogue and I should have known better: Reform Jews (known in England as "liberals") have been optionally topless in synagogue for over half a century. All the same, the contrast between unctuous performance of ritual and selective departure from established traditions struck me then and strikes me now as a clue to the compensatory quality of American Jewish identity.

S ome years ago I attended a gala benefit dinner in Manhattan for prominent celebrities in the arts and journalism. Halfway through the ceremonies, a middle-aged man leaned across the table and glared at me: "Are you Tony Judt? You really must stop writing these terrible things about Israel!" Primed for such interrogations, I asked him what was so terrible about what I had written. "I don't know. You may be right—I've never been to Israel. But we Jews must stick together: we may need Israel one day." The return of eliminationist anti-Semitism was just a matter of time: New York might become unlivable.

I find it odd—and told him so—that American Jews should have taken out a territorial insurance policy in the Middle East lest we find ourselves back in Poland in 1942. But even more curious was the setting for this exchange: the overwhelming majority of the awardees that evening were Jewish. Jews in America are more successful, integrated, respected, and influential than at any place or time in the history of the community. Why then is contemporary Jewish identity in the US so obsessively attached to the recollection—and anticipation—of its own disappearance?

Had Hitler never happened, Judaism might indeed have fallen into deliquescence. With the breakdown of Jewish isolation in the course of the later nineteenth century throughout much of Europe, the religious, communitarian, and ritualistic boundaries of Judaism were eroding: centuries of ignorance and mutually enforced separation were coming to a close. Assimilation—by migration, marriage, and cultural dilution—was well underway.

In retrospect, the interim consequences can be confusing. In Germany, many Jews thought of themselves as Germans—and were resented for just that reason. In Central Europe, notably in the unrepresentative urban triangle of Prague-Budapest-Vienna, a secularized Jewish intelligentsia—influential in the liberal professions—established a distinctive basis for postcommunitarian Jewish life. But the world of Kafka, Kraus, and Zweig was brittle: dependent upon the unique circumstances of a disintegrating liberal empire, it was helpless in the face of the tempests of ethnonationalism. For those in search of cultural roots, it offers little beyond regret and nostalgia. The dominant trajectory for Jews in those years was assimilation.

I can see this in my own family. My grandparents came out of the shtetl and into unfriendly alien environments—an experience that temporarily reinforced a defensive Jewish self-awareness. But for their children, those same environments represented normal life. My parents' generation of European Jews neglected their Yiddish, frustrated the expectations of their immigrant families, and spurned communitarian rituals and restrictions. As late as the 1930s, it was reasonable to suppose that their own children—my generation—would be left with little more than a handful of memories of "the old country": something like the pasta-and-St.-Patrick's-Day nostalgia of Italian-Americans or Irish-Americans, and with about as much meaning.

But things turned out differently. A generation of emancipated young Jews, many of whom had fondly imagined themselves fully integrated into a post-communitarian world, was forcibly re-introduced to Judaism as civic identity: one that they were no longer free to decline. Religion—once the foundation of Jewish experience—was pushed ever further to the margin. In Hitler's wake, Zionism (hitherto a sectarian minority preference) became a realistic option. Jewishness became a secular attribute, externally attributed.

Ever since, Jewish identity in contemporary America has had a curious dybbuk-like quality: it lives on by virtue of a double, near-death experience. The result is a sensitivity to past suffering that can appear disproportionate even to fellow Jews. Shortly after publishing an essay on Israel's future, I was invited to London for an interview with *The Jewish Chronicle*—the local Jewish paper of record. I went with trepidation, anticipating further aspersions upon my imperfect identification with the Chosen People. To my surprise, the editor turned off the microphone: "Before we start," she began, "I'd like to ask you something. How can you stand to live among those awful American Jews?"

And yet, maybe those "awful American Jews" are onto something despite themselves. For what can it mean— following the decline of faith, the abatement of persecution, and the fragmentation of community—to insist upon one's Jewishness? A "Jewish" state where one has no intention of living and whose intolerant clerisy excludes ever more Jews from official recognition? An "ethnic" membership criterion that one would be embarrassed to invoke for any other purpose?

There was a time when being Jewish was a lived condition. In the US today, religion no longer defines us: just 46 percent of Jews belong to a synagogue, only 27 percent attend at least once a month, and no more than 21 percent of the synagogue members (10 percent of the whole) are Orthodox. In short, the "old believers" are but a minority.[1] Modern-day Jews live on preserved memory. Being Jewish largely consists of remembering what it once meant to be Jewish. Indeed, of all the rabbinical injunctions, the most enduring and distinctive is *Zakhor!*—Remember! But most Jews have internalized this injunction without any very secure sense of what it requires of them. We are the people who remember . . . something.

What, then, should we remember? Great-grandma's

latkes back in Pilvistock? I doubt it: shorn of setting and symbols, they are nothing but apple cakes. Childhood tales of Cossack terrors (I recall them well)? What possible resonance could these have to a generation who has never known a Cossack? Memory is a poor foundation for any collective enterprise. The authority of historical injunction, lacking contemporary iteration, grows obscure.

In this sense, American Jews are instinctively correct to indulge their Holocaust obsession: it provides reference, liturgy, example, and moral instruction—as well as historical proximity. And yet they are making a terrible mistake: they have confused a means of remembering with a reason to do so. Are we really Jews for no better reason than that Hitler sought to exterminate our grandparents? If we fail to rise above this consideration, our grandchildren will have little cause to identify with us.

In Israel today, the Holocaust is officially invoked as a reminder of how hateful non-Jews can be. Its commemoration in the diaspora is doubly exploited: to justify uncompromising Israelophilia and to service lachrymose self-regard. This seems to me a vicious abuse of memory. But what if the Holocaust served instead to bring us closer, so far as possible, to a truer understanding of the tradition we evoke?

Here, remembering becomes part of a broader social obligation by no means confined to Jews. We acknowledge readily enough our duties to our contemporaries; but what of our obligations to those who came before us? We talk glibly of

what we owe the future—but what of our debt to the past?
Except in crassly practical ways—preserving institutions or
edifices—we can only service that debt to the full by remembering and conveying beyond ourselves the duty to remember.

Unlike my table companion, I don't expect Hitler to return. And I refuse to remember his crimes as an occasion to
close off conversation: to repackage Jewishness as a defensive
indifference to doubt or self-criticism and a retreat into self-
pity. I choose to invoke a Jewish past that is impervious to
orthodoxy: that opens conversations rather than closes them.
Judaism for me is a sensibility of collective self-questioning
and uncomfortable truth-telling: the *dafka*-like[2] quality of
awkwardness and dissent for which we were once known. It
is not enough to stand at a tangent to other peoples' conven-
tions; we should also be the most unforgiving critics of our
own. I feel a debt of responsibility to this past. It is why I am
Jewish.

Toni Avegael was transported to Auschwitz in 1942 and
gassed to death there as a Jew. I am named after her.

1. See the National Jewish Population Survey 2000–01, p. 7; see http://
www.jewishfederations.org/getfile.asp?id=3905.
2. *Dafka*: contrarian.

ENVOI

XXV

Magic Mountains

One is not supposed to love Switzerland. Express-
ing affection for the Swiss or their country is
akin to confessing nostalgia for cigarette smoking or *The
Brady Bunch*. It immediately brands you as someone at once
unforgivably ignorant of the developments of the past thirty
years and incurably conventional in the worst way. Whenever I blurt out my weakness for the place the young yawn
politely, liberal colleagues look askance ("Don't you *know*
about the War?"), my family smiles indulgently: Oh, *that*
again! I don't care. I love Switzerland.

What are the objections? Well, Switzerland means
mountains. But if it is Alps you want, the French have higher,
you eat better in Italy, and snow comes cheaper in Austria.
Most damning of all, people are friendlier in Germany. As for

TONY JUDT

the Swiss themselves, "Brotherly love, five hundred years of democracy and peace, and what did they produce? The cuckoo clock."

It gets worse. Switzerland did remarkably well out of World War II—trading with Berlin and laundering looted assets. It was the Swiss who urged Hitler to mark Jewish passports with a "J"—and who, in an embarrassing exercise in recidivist chauvinism, have just voted to ban minaret construction (in a country that has only four and where almost all resident Muslims are secular Bosnian refugees). Then there are the tax evaders, although it has never been clear to me just why what Swiss banks do in servicing a handful of wealthy foreign criminals is significantly worse than what Goldman Sachs has done with the proceeds of millions of honest US tax dollars.

So why do I like it? In the first place, the country has the virtues of its defects. Dull? To be sure. But dull can also translate as safe, tidy, clean. A few years ago I flew to Geneva with my younger son, then nine years old. Upon arrival, we descended to the railway station—one of those that the Swiss so boringly locate directly underneath their airports—and sat down in a café to await our train. "It's so clean!" the little boy observed. And so it was: obtrusively pristine. Unremarkable, perhaps, if you come from Singapore or Liechtenstein—but not to a child raised on JFK and whose only experience of a European airport until then had been confined to the tatty shopping mall at Heathrow.

The Swiss are obsessed with cleanliness. Once, on a train out of Interlaken, I was upbraided by an elderly lady for briefly placing the outer edge of my left foot on the corner of the seat facing me. In England, where no one would have noticed or cared, I might well have been taken aback at such brazen interference. But in Switzerland I merely felt embarrassed at having broken such an obvious civic code—implicated as I was in a shared responsibility for public good. It is irritating to be called to order by one's fellow citizens, but in the long run their callous indifference does far more harm.

Switzerland is a striking instance of the possibilities—and, therefore, the benefits—of blended identities. By this I do not mean the mixture of languages (German, French, Italian, Romansch), or the striking—and often neglected—topographical variety. I mean contrast. Everything in Germany is efficient, so there is no variety to nourish the soul. Italy is unremittingly interesting: there is no relief. But Switzerland is full of contrasts: efficient but provincial; beautiful but bland; hospitable but charmless—at least to the foreigners on whom it depends for so much of its well-being.

The contrast that matters most is that between the fickle surface sheen and the steady depths below. A few summers ago I took a trip to the summit of the Klein Matterhorn, a popular glacier skiing resort above Zermatt. There on the sun-dappled slopes—decorating the benches of an absurdly expensive restaurant—assorted Italian floozettes in micro-kinis and fur booties were draped across hard-faced Russians helicoptered to the summit sporting the latest gear. *Debbie Does Davos*: Switzerland at its worst.

And then, as out of nowhere, there appeared around the corner three little old men: swathed in wool and leather, their ruddy, sensible-looking faces topped by sensible-looking hats. Hands firmly gripping stout climbing sticks, they plumped their substantial backsides onto a bench and unlaced their weathered boots. Sublimely indifferent to the dolce vita unfolding before them, the gnarled mountaineers congratulated one another in incomprehensible Switzerdeutsch on what must have been a grueling ascent—and, sweating profusely, ordered three beers from the cheerful, white-bodiced waitress: the good Switzerland.

During the 1950s, my parents and I took a number of trips to Switzerland. This was their brief parenthetical moment of prosperity, but in any case Switzerland then was not so very expensive. I think what struck me as a child was the uncluttered *regularity* of everything. We usually arrived via France, in those days a poor and run-down country. French village houses were still pockmarked with shell damage, their Dubonnet ads torn and crumbling. The food was good (even a London schoolboy could tell that) but the restaurants and hotels had a damp, tumble-down air to them: cheap and cheerless.

And then you crossed the border, always at some wind-swept, snow-drenched pass or summit . . . and entered a land of neat, flower-bedecked chalets, air-brushed streets, prosperous-looking shops, and smart, satisfied citizens. Switzerland seemed so untouched by the war that had just ended. Mine was a black-and-white childhood, but Switzerland came in color: red and white, brown and green, yellow and gold. And the hotels! The Swiss hotels of my childhood evoked fresh pine, as though they had sprung organically from the surrounding forests. There was warm, solid wood everywhere: thick wooden doors, padded wooden staircases, firm wooden beds, chirping wooden clocks.

The dining rooms had large picture windows, there were flowers and crisp white linens galore—and although this cannot be true, it seems to me as I think back that there was no one else around. I, of course, had never heard of Clavdia Chauchat; but in later years I would imagine her sweeping silently into one of those dining rooms, her dark eyes scanning the tables, while I—Castorp-like—silently entreated her to join me. In actuality, my companions were stolid-looking couples of a certain age: Switzerland lets you dream, but only so much.

Memory plays tricks. I know that we almost always spent our holidays in the Bernese Oberland: German-speaking Switzerland. Yet I associate the country fondly with my first stumbling efforts to speak French: choosing chocolate, asking directions, learning to ski. And buying tickets. Switzerland for me has always been about trains: their distinctive virtues seductively encapsulated in the little transport museum just outside Luzern. Here one learns of the first electric trains in the world; the first and most technically accomplished rail tunnels; the highest railways in Europe—culminating in the astonishing Jungfraujochbahn driven up through the heart of the Eiger and terminating at a permanent station 11,225 feet above sea level.

The Swiss, curiously, are never troubled by what British Rail used to call "the wrong kind of leaves"—or, indeed, the wrong kind of snow. Just as the little mountain men ascend the daunting Klein Matterhorn with an untroubled air, so the trains that their great-grandfathers built have for decades trundled effortlessly up and down from Brig to Zermatt, from Chur to St. Moritz, from Bex to Villars.

At Andermatt, the epicenter of the country where the Rhine and Rhône rivers surge icily out of their mountain fastness, the Milan–Zurich *transalpini* slice deep into the Gotthard mountains while hundreds of feet above them the Glacier Express cuts a series of terrifying switchback cog tracks on its vertiginous climb clear over the roof of Europe. It is hard enough to navigate these routes in a car, much less cycle or walk them. How on earth were they built? Who are these people?

My happiest memories are of Mürren. We first went

there when I was eight years old: an unspoiled village halfway up the Schilthorn massif attainable only by rack railway or cable car. It takes forever—and a minimum of four trains—to reach the place, and there is little to do once you arrive. There is no particularly good food and the shopping is unexciting, to say the least.

The skiing, I am told, is good; the walking certainly is. The views—across a deep valley to the Jungfrau chain—are spectacular. The nearest thing to entertainment is the clockwork-like arrival and departure of the little single-carriage train that wends its way around the mountainside to the head of the *funiculaire*. The electric *whoosh* as it starts out of the tiny station and the reassuring clunk of the rails are the nearest thing to noise pollution in the village. With the last engine safely in its shed, the plateau falls silent.

In 2002, in the wake of an operation for cancer and a month of heavy radiation, I took my family back to Mürren. My sons, aged eight and six, seemed to me to experience the place just as I had, even though we stayed in a distinctly better class of hotel. They drank hot chocolate, clambered across open fields of mountain flowers and tiny waterfalls, stared moonstruck at the great Eiger—and reveled in the little railway. Unless I was very much mistaken, Mürren itself had not changed at all, and there was still nothing to do. Paradise.

I have never thought of myself as a rooted person. We are born by chance in one town rather than another and pass through various temporary homes in the course of our vagrant lives—at least that is how it has been for me. Most places hold mixed memories: I cannot think of Cambridge or Paris or Oxford or New York without recalling a kaleidoscope of encounters and experiences. How I remember them varies with my mood. But Mürren never changes. Nothing ever went wrong there.

There is a path of sorts that accompanies Mürren's pocket railway. Halfway along, a little café—the only stop on the line—serves the usual run of Swiss wayside fare. Ahead, the mountain falls steeply away into the rift valley below. Behind, you can clamber up to the summer barns with the cows and goats and shepherds. Or you can just wait for the next train: punctual, predictable, and precise to the second. Nothing happens: it is the happiest place in the world. We cannot choose where we start out in life, but we may finish where we will. I know where I shall be: going nowhere in particular on that little train, forever and ever.